MIDDLE – FINGER MANAGEMENT

A SARCASTIC SURVIVAL GUIDE TO TOXIC BOSSES, STOLEN CREDIT, AND CORPORATE CHAOS

∽⚬∽

C. V. WOOSTER

Published By:

Published by TaciturnStudios.com – Taciturn Studios LLC, Los Angeles, CA, USA

Printed in the United States of America

First Printing Edition, 2025

ISBN 979-8-9919148-4-0

Dedication

To **MA, SC, TB, SE**, and all the many **Middle Finger Managers** who made this book possible—not by supporting me, but by relentlessly demonstrating exactly **how not to lead, how not to inspire, and how not to be decent human beings**.

Your insufferable micromanagement, your oblivious power trips, your complete and utter inability to read a room - these were the gifts that kept on giving. Without your **convoluted policies, last - minute demands, and inspirational emails dripping with corporate gaslighting**, I might have remained blissfully ignorant of the depths of professional absurdity. But instead, you sharpened my wit, strengthened my resilience, and, most importantly, provided **an endless supply of material**.

To the **email warriors** who cc'd half the company just to prove a point, the **meeting - addicted bureaucrats** who insisted we "circle back" on things that never needed circling in the first place, and the **self - proclaimed visionaries** who thought "engagement tracking spreadsheets" were the solution to all of life's problems—this one's for you.

May your **LinkedIn posts** be filled with **vague leadership buzzwords**, may your **team - building exercises** remain universally despised, and may you one day experience the joy of actually **listening** to the people who work for you.

I won't hold my breath.

Contents

Author's Note

If you've made it this far, congratulations - you clearly have the patience for absurdity, the endurance for prolonged exposure to dysfunction, and perhaps even a sense of humor dark enough to survive the modern world. Good. You'll need all of that.

This book is not for the faint of heart, the easily offended, or those who believe life should follow a neatly structured, color - coded timeline with predictable outcomes. If you're looking for **a heartwarming tale of overcoming adversity through sheer grit and positive thinking, kindly exit stage left.** This is not that book.

What you're about to read is **messy, raw, sometimes uncomfortable, and occasionally funny in the way that a well - timed disaster can be.** It's about autism, trauma, survival, and the long - running circus act that is human interaction. It's also about resilience—not the buzzword kind that corporate stooges like to toss around in staff meetings, but the real kind: the **"I've seen some shit, and yet here I am"** kind.

There are no sweeping Hollywood redemption arcs here, no profound moments of enlightenment where everything magically falls into place. **Life doesn't work that way.** But if there's a thread that runs through this book, it's this: **survival is an art form.** And sometimes, the greatest act of rebellion is simply **refusing to disappear.**

So, read on. Or don't. I'm not your boss, and I certainly won't be tracking your engagement. But if you do, just know that every word was written with the same attitude that got me through it all: a middle finger in one hand and a pen in the other.

Introduction:
The Reality of Middle - Finger Management

Congratulations, you must have a crappy boss! Or at least you survived one at your last job before you got fired for daring to use, of all things, ... common sense. Or maybe you've just reached your limit with office politics and passive - aggressive emails. Either way, welcome to the club—you're in the right place. You've finally had it with those tiny dictators who think they're running the show just because they've got a fancy title, a bad haircut, and a Napoleon complex. Carlos Castaneda, the anthropologist and author, called them "petty tyrants," but let's be real—they're just annoying coworkers who desperately need a reality check and a decent barber.

In this book, we'll refer to these characters as Middle - Finger Managers, MFs, Fingers, or just Middles. So, how do you deal with these mini - Hitlers without losing your mind, your job, or your will to live? First, take a deep breath and remember: they're compensating for something. Maybe a bad childhood, a failed marriage, or a receding hairline. The point is, they're not going to suddenly develop self - awareness and apologize for being a pain in the butt.

So, put on your best "I'm interested" face, nod along, and let them drone on while you mentally redecorate your living room or count down to a happy hour. Petty tyrants are like that one aunt at family reunions—always drama - llama - ing about something. When they start micromanaging or stealing your ideas, simply smile and say, "I am delighted that you like my idea! Can I put your name on it too?" Trust me, it's like throwing water on a grease fire—it'll either put out the flames or make them look like a total idiot.

Ah, the Middle - Finger Managers—the ones who act like they've ascended Mount Olympus because they've got a few extra letters on their business card. These wannabe Napoleons are practically fueled by fear: fear of being unmasked as the frauds they are, fear of losing control, fear that someone competent will expose them. They hide behind a facade of authority, making everyone around them miserable in their quest to maintain their shaky grip on power.

We've all been there. Sitting in a meeting where your manager spouts buzzwords and corporate jargon like they're auditioning for a TED Talk, knowing full well they don't have a clue. Or maybe it's those dismissive remarks that cut into your sense of worth: "We're looking for someone really innovative," as if you've been doodling for the past five years. Or, god forbid, they want to "run it up the flagpole to see who salutes" and/or the dreaded "circle back later" in order to review their amazing command decision that was probably someone else's idea in the first place.

Let's not forget, meetings—the corporate version of waterboarding, but with more Google Slides. Nothing quite says "waste of a perfectly good morning" like being herded into a conference room (or worse, a mandatory Zoom call) so your Middle-Finger Manager can flex their "leadership skills" by talking in circles for an hour.

And let's be honest, the agenda is a lie. It's a list of things that theoretically should be discussed but will inevitably be hijacked by your MF droning on about synergy, leveraging assets, and "thinking outside the box"—which is ironic because you're pretty sure the box is your cubicle and you're trapped in it. And don't even get me started on the mandatory "let's go around the room and share" moment—a glorified hostage situation where you have to pretend to be engaged while mentally composing your resignation letter.

But the real insult? The "quick" meeting that drags on for eternity. You know the one. It starts with your MF promising "this won't take long", which is corporate code for 'cancel your lunch plans and say goodbye to your will to live'. By the time it's over, nothing has been accomplished, you've lost three brain cells and half a workday, and your MF is beaming like they just cured cancer, completely unaware that everyone in the room is plotting their downfall. And somehow, despite all that, there will be ANOTHER meeting next week. Because if there's one thing MFs love more than power trips, it's subjecting you to more meetings about meetings. And let's be frank, meetings deserve a book unto themselves. I smell sequel!

But here's the truth: these MFs don't have any real power. They might hold your paycheck and workload, but they don't control you. They're just scared little kings of tiny, pathetic kingdoms. Once you see them for what they are, their power starts to fade. Surviving these Middle - Fingers is like navigating an obstacle course of office politics and passive - aggressive comments. They drain your energy, sap your creativity, and make you question your sanity. They'll keep you up at night, replaying that one pointless conversation where they shot down your idea without even listening. Spoiler alert: it's not you. It's them.

So, what can you expect from this book? We're going to dive into the world of MFs, dissecting their behavior and finding ways to navigate their chaos. You'll read stories from my own life, like being stabbed in the back with a metaphorical ice cream scoop—Hershey syrup bleeding out of my ego. We'll explore why these people seem to rise to the top, how they make others miserable, and most importantly—how to survive and even thrive in a world filled with these petty tyrants.

Want to know the secret to dealing with Middles? It's not about avoiding them altogether (although that sounds like a dream). The real challenge is surviving them long enough to realize their toxic behavior is not your problem. They'll try to drain your energy and crush your creativity, but you'll learn how to flip the script. We'll explore what makes them tick, laugh at their absurdity, and give you tools to navigate their world without losing your sanity. So buckle up; it's time to take back your power!!!

Chapter 01:
Anatomy of a Middle - Finger

Let's face it: Middle - Fingers are an inevitable part of the modern workplace. These managers, or MFs for short (and yes, that conveniently stands for Mother F****, which feels oddly appropriate), are the reason your blood pressure spikes every time your phone buzzes with a work email. They aren't just bad bosses; they're walking, talking examples of how mediocrity can climb the corporate ladder and pull the rug out from under everyone else. You'll spot them in any field—corporate offices, retail, education, you name it—wearing their incompetence like a badge of honor, complete with a participation trophy and a "World's Okayest Boss" mug. They're like the human version of a participation trophy, minus the actual participation.

Ah, yes. Middle - Fingers all share the same predictable anatomy. It's practically genetic. They're ambidextrous, which in their case means they can stab you in the back with either hand—how versatile! It's like evolution gave them this special skill just to keep things interesting. And let's not forget their voices. Oh, their voices. If nails on a chalkboard could breed with a kazoo, you'd get the sweet symphony of a Middle - Finger's vocal cords. Whether they're mumbling incoherently or bellowing orders, their mere existence is guaranteed to get your blood boiling. And whispers? Please. These guys wouldn't know subtlety if it danced naked in front of them. They're genetically predisposed to bombastic outbursts, so if you're hoping for a quiet day at the office, think again.

Oh, and did I mention their double - jointed flexibility? It's not just for show. This talent helps them perform Olympic - level backflips when it comes to dodging responsibility. They can twist and contort reality so skillfully, you'd think they moonlight as circus performers.

Their other peculiar anatomy is next on our list:

Sight:

Middle - Fingers possess a special kind of vision, one that's finely tuned to zero in on every mistake you've ever made, while conveniently blurring out their own faults. It's like their eyes come with built - in selective focus. They can spot a typo in your email from across the room but somehow miss that they've approved a project that's completely off - budget. Their eyes are also great at avoiding eye contact during crucial conversations, like when it's time to discuss that promotion they promised you last year. In those moments, their gaze suddenly becomes fascinated with the ceiling, the floor, or the back of their own eyelids.

Hearing:

Oh, they have excellent hearing... when it comes to gossip. But when you need to discuss something important, like, I don't know, the fact that the office is on fire? Suddenly, it's like you're speaking in an alien language. Their ears are programmed to pick up on office drama, passive - aggressive compliments, and anything that lets them eavesdrop on your conversations. But constructive feedback? Requests for help? Ha! Your words might as well be transmitted through a tin can and string.

Touch:

Middle - Fingers have an uncanny ability to lay a hand on every project, task, or decision and make it worse. Their touch is not the Midas touch—more like the "everything I touch turns into a bureaucratic nightmare" touch. They don't actually do any of the work, mind you, but they sure do love to get their greasy little fingerprints all over your hard - earned accomplishments. Also, they have a knack for finding your metaphorical jugular and squeezing just enough to keep you uncomfortable but not enough to let you quit without a fight.

MFs Interference Outcomes

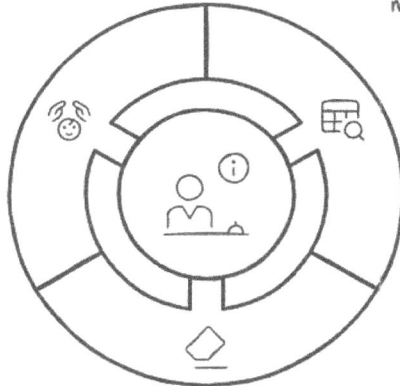

Emotional Manipulation
Pressure tactics that create tension

Micromanagement
Overbearing oversight that complicates projects

Bureaucratic Red Tape
Unnecessary processes that hinder progress

Smell:

Ah, the olfactory senses of a Middle - Finger. Somehow, they are completely immune to the stench of their own incompetence but have an acute sense for sniffing out any whiff of rebellion or dissatisfaction in the office. The moment you have a thought that's even remotely rebellious or defiant, you can bet they'll be standing at your desk asking, "Everything okay?" with that insincere smile that's one passive - aggressive breath away from making you lose it.

Taste:

No one appreciates the bitter taste of taking credit for someone else's hard work quite like a Middle - Finger. It's their favorite dish. They feast on your ideas, your overtime, and your innovative solutions like they're a Michelin - starred meal. And the best part? They wash it down with the sweet satisfaction of watching you squirm as they present your work as their own in the next meeting.

Brainpower:

Ah, yes, the Middle - Finger brain. Now, you might think this is where things would go awry, but no. Middle - Fingers possess an incredible talent for mental gymnastics. They can twist logic to justify every terrible decision, deny responsibility for any failure, and still manage to pat themselves on the back for a job well done. Their brains are wired for self - preservation above all else. They can recall every detail of a mistake you made five years ago, but when asked to explain why they approved that disastrous initiative last week? Oh, suddenly they can't recall. Selective amnesia, it seems, is just another part of their anatomy.

Gut Instincts:

Funny thing about Middle - Fingers—they never trust their gut. They rely entirely on convoluted processes, committee decisions, and endless red tape to avoid having to actually make a choice themselves. If they do follow their gut, it's usually after at least six layers of management and three consultants have sufficiently massaged it. And even then, if it goes wrong, well, they never trusted their gut in the first place, right?

So, there you have it—the full anatomical breakdown of the Middle - Finger. They're more than just irritating bosses. They're an entire species of office creatures with finely honed, self - serving adaptations designed to ensure their survival while driving you completely up the wall. But fear not, dear reader. This book is your field guide to navigating their world - and maybe even coming out on top.

So how does this play out in real - life? Here's a story about my first experience with a Middle - Finger. I was 16, scooping ice cream at Baskin - Robbins, where the only thing more plentiful than the sprinkles was my naivety. It was my first job, and I had big dreams for myself. Management material, I thought, as I clicked the register closed and flipped the sign to "Closed" on my first solo night shift. I was proud. Until the next day, when I walked in, my chest puffed up with accomplishment, and was promptly shown the door. No more brown - and - pink uniform, no more ice cream scooper in hand. Fired. Just like that. I was left wondering if I'd accidentally superglued my shoes to the floor because it felt like I'd been stuck in place while the world moved on without me. I had visions of my future self, stuck in a never - ending cycle of minimum - wage jobs, all because of one fateful encounter with a Middle - Finger. The horror!

The reason? Bananas. Or rather, the lack of them. Turns out, we ran out of bananas for the banana splits, and one of the owner's family members—good old Uncle Charlie—was horrified. I mean, who doesn't love a good banana split? It's like the ultimate comfort food. But I digress. Now, understand, I didn't know that I was supposed to run across the street to buy more. I was sixteen, trained by a guy with a peach - fuzz mustache, barely older than me, who never once mentioned that keeping the banana supply flowing was a matter of life and death. It was like being thrown into a war zone without a map or a compass. So, instead of being told what to do, I was blamed for something I didn't even know was part of my job. It was like being accused of stealing the last slice of pizza without even knowing there was pizza in the first place.

I remember standing there that night we ran out of ice cream's favorite produce, frozen in shock, as Uncle Charlie's face turned beet red with rage. His voice was like thunder, and I was the poor little ant about to get squashed. I thought to myself, "This is it. I'm going to get written up or called into the office the size of a chest freezer in the back room and told to never let it happen again. "The thought sent a chill down my spine, and I felt my heart sink to the floor. It was like watching a slow - motion train wreck, and I was the helpless bystander. This, it appeared, was an offence against all humanity. An ice cream store with no bananas. Grown men were weeping all over the world because of my banana faux pas (not a bad name for a new frozen treat – bananas faux pas, kinda rolls off the tongue much like bananas foster). But Uncle Charlie had sealed my fate. A paper write - up or finger - wag was too logical. No, this required true retribution and 'Charlie the executioner' sealed my fate that night as his familial pressure bore down on my manager, 'professor peach - fuzz'.

It was a crash course in Middle - Finger Syndrome (MFS)—my very first one. And here's what I learned: MFs thrive on power and control, but that control is fragile. They need to project authority because, deep down, they know they're unqualified or unprepared. They'll never admit they messed up. Instead, they'll throw you under the bus at the first opportunity. And there I was, lying flat under the wheels, syrupy from head to toe with Hershey's syrup as a farewell gift. Few prisoners with lengthy rap sheets had been shanked more than me that night, I reasoned. Gutted by an ice cream scooper, of all things. Oh, the humanity?! I felt like I'd been robbed of my innocence, my dignity, and my ice cream - scooping skills all at once.

Fast - forward decades later, and I found myself in a classroom, teaching bright young minds. Or trying to, anyway, despite being horribly sick with allergies one fateful day. My eyes were swollen, my nose was a waterfall of misery, and my ability to form coherent thoughts was on the fritz. The plan was simple: go home early and recover. But, just as I was packing up, my administrator—let's call him Mr. Big Shot—decided this was the perfect time for an unannounced classroom evaluation. I mean, who doesn't love a good ambush? It's like the ultimate test of a teacher's mettle. But I digress. The sad part is, I had emailed him earlier in the day to tell him I was going home. But before my substitute arrived to take over for the last period of the day, Mr. BS was on the case. Here I was, seemingly in an old west shootout with the sheriff and me dueling it out on Main Street. Only this time, it was Mr. Big Shot versus Mr. Big Snot.

Imagine trying to engage students while your face is a mucus - filled mess. I don't remember much about the lesson, except that I survived. Barely. It was like trying to deliver a TED Talk while drowning in a sea of snot and tears. Mr. Big Shot didn't care that I was visibly unwell. He didn't care that I'd already explained I was going home early. He cared about his power move: catching me at my weakest and flexing his evaluative muscles. It's the hallmark of MFS. They prey on vulnerability, needing to feel superior, even if it means kicking you while you're down.

I recall feeling like I was in a nightmare, with Mr. Big Shot playing the role of the villainous taskmaster. He was determined to make an example out of me, to show the entire school that he was the one in charge. And I was just a pawn in his game of power and control. The students, bless their hearts, were probably more concerned about my health than the lesson itself. But Mr. Big Shot didn't care about that. He only cared about his own ego and his need to assert dominance.

And that evaluation? It stuck with me. Permanently. A black mark on my teaching record because I didn't deliver an Oscar - worthy lesson while sneezing into my sleeve. Mr. Big Shot made sure of it, probably puffing out his chest like he'd just scored a win in some kind of petty office Olympics. I felt like I'd been robbed of my dignity, my pride, and my ability to breathe through my nose all at once.

But here's the thing: every time you face a Middle - Finger, you learn a little more about how to deal with them. At first, they seem like these all - powerful beings, capable of ruining your day, your job, and your life. But the more you understand their game, the more you see the cracks. Their power is an illusion, built on their insecurities and fear of being exposed as frauds. They throw people under the bus because it's easier than admitting they don't know what they're doing. It's like they're trying to prove a point, but the only point they're proving is that they're desperate for control.

I've come to realize that dealing with a Middle - Finger is like suiting up for battle. I picture myself as Don Quixote, charging at the windmills of management nonsense every day. I know they'll try to stop me—they always do. Whether it's rewriting a project at the last minute, springing an unexpected meeting, or taking credit for your work, they're masters of sabotage. But once you start to expect it, you stop letting it affect you. You find the humor in it. You start to see the absurdity of their actions, and that's when you gain the upper hand.

It's a delicate balance, really. You have to take their antics seriously enough to prepare for them, but not so seriously that you let them get under your skin. And that's the key to surviving in a world filled with Middle - Fingers: learning to laugh at their antics and never giving them the satisfaction of getting a rise out of you.

Take the time I was about to present a well - researched project I'd been working on for months. I was ready. My team was ready. Then, out of nowhere, my MF manager strolls in and says, "You know, I think we should take this in a different direction." Mind you, this is right before I'm supposed to present it. Different direction? What does that even mean? Suddenly, the whole project is up in the air because Mr. Middle - Finger has a "gut feeling."

Understanding the Middle-Finger Syndrome in the Workplace

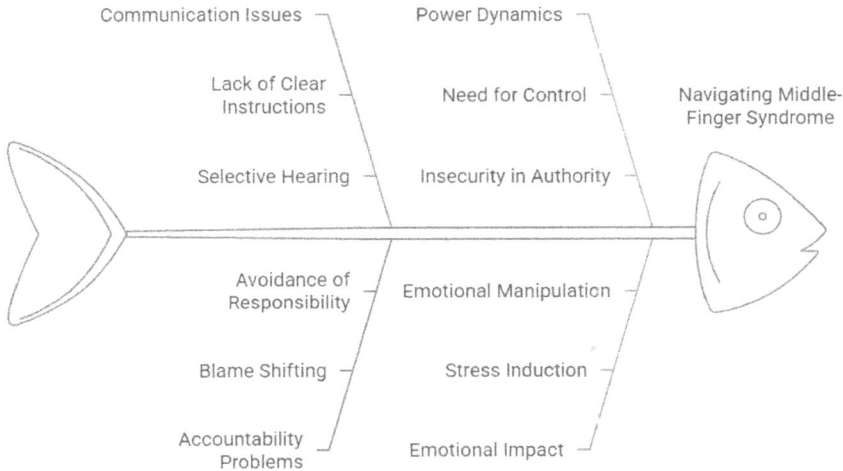

Communication Issues

Lack of Clear
Instructions

Power Dynamics

Need for Control

Navigating Middle-
Finger Syndrome

Selective Hearing

Insecurity in Authority

Avoidance of
Responsibility

Emotional Manipulation

Blame Shifting

Stress Induction

Accountability
Problems

Emotional Impact

That's the thing with MFs. It's always about control. Whether it's controlling the project, the narrative, or your job itself, they thrive on holding power over you. They're like puppet masters, pulling the strings to make you dance to their tune. But here's the secret I've learned: their behavior is often a reflection of the chaos they're trying to keep at bay in their own lives. They're desperate to maintain their little kingdoms because they know, deep down, they're not really qualified to run them. They're like impostors, trying to fake it until they make it, but ultimately, they're just winging it.

It's a classic case of the emperor's new clothes, where everyone is too afraid to speak up and say, "Hey, you're not wearing any clothes!" But once you realize that, you can start to see through their facade. You can start to call their bluff, and that's when the power dynamic shifts. That's when you take back control, and they're left standing there, exposed like the naked emperors they really are.

Once you realize that, everything changes. Their power starts to fade because you start to see through the façade. Sure, they're still annoying, but at least you can start to find humor in the absurdity. Because what else can you do? You could rage against the machine, but at the end of the day, laughing at the ridiculousness is a lot more fun—and a lot better for your blood pressure. It's now a bad parody of a leader, where they're trying to be taken seriously but are really just making a mockery of themselves.

The thing about MFS is that it's so widespread, I bet you're nodding along right now. Maybe you're thinking of that one manager who loved to schedule "urgent" meetings at 4:45 p.m. on a Friday. Or the boss who seemed to only remember your name when there was a credit to steal or blame to pass. We've all been there, and it's a relief to know you're not alone.

What's important is that you recognize their game. Middle - Fingers thrive on chaos and confusion. But once you know their tricks, it's like the curtain has been pulled back to a bad magician fumble through his routine. You can't help but laugh at how obvious the sleight of hand is. You start to see the patterns, the tactics they use to manipulate and control. And once you see it, you can't unsee it. The illusion is shattered, and you're left with a sense of empowerment, knowing that you're no longer falling for their tricks.

So, the next time your Middle - Finger starts throwing around veiled threats or pulling power moves, remember, they're not as powerful as they seem. They're just really good at pretending. And once you see through the act, surviving their toxic reign becomes a lot more manageable. You start to realize that their bark is worse than their bite, and that they're just trying to intimidate you into submission.

This, my friend, is just the beginning. As we will see, there are more MFs to meet, more stories to share, and more lessons to learn. Buckle up— it's going to be a bumpy ride, but at least we can laugh along the way.

∿

Chapter 02:
Cost of Toxic Leadership

You're not crazy; your job really is that bad. I mean, it's not like you're being dramatic or overly sensitive, right? Nope—you're a perfectly sane, well - adjusted human being. It's just that your Middle - Finger Manager (MF for short)[1] has turned your work life into a caffeine - fueled nightmare, forcing you to gulp down coffee like it's an Olympic sport while daydreaming about quitting to become a professional hammock tester or a part - time alpaca farmer in the Andes. Not because you're weak or can't handle the stress, but because your MF has honed the fine art of driving you insane into a cruel science. They know exactly which buttons to press, which levers to pull, and when to throw a wrench in the works, just to see how much more of your soul they can extract before you completely lose it.

Think about it: When was the last time you actually felt like a rock star at work? When was the last time your MF complimented you without making you wonder if the apocalypse was upon us? Oh, wait, what's that? Never? Yeah, sounds about right. MFs are like dementors from *Harry Potter*, except instead of sucking your soul out through your face, they drain you of every ounce of confidence you once had. Compliments? Oh, please. The

---

[1]   https://tera-allas.medium.com/the-boss-factor-at-play-bosses-impact-on-life-satisfaction-ed40fcae05ec#:~:text=Both%20the%20measures%20I've,lot%20of%20it%20out%20there

closest you'll ever get to a compliment from an MF is something like, "Well, at least you didn't mess this up as badly as last time." Yeah, thanks for that pep talk, boss. Real confidence boost.

And don't even get me started on their "constructive criticism." You know, the type that makes you feel as though you are one bad email away from being immediately terminated. It's like they've gone to night school for "How to Break Your Employees in 5 Easy Steps." "You're not meeting expectations." "This isn't up to par." "You're just not cut out for this." Well, excuse me, Karen, but maybe if you provided actual feedback instead of vague insults wrapped in corporate speak, I wouldn't be mentally composing my resignation letter during our 9 a.m. "team meeting."

But guess what? **It's not you. It's them**[2]. They're the problem. They're broken, like that squeaky office chair you've been trying to get replaced for the last six months. MFs are so insecure and terrified that you will surpass them that they must undermine you at every opportunity. It's not just toxic—it's textbook insecurity in action. The real kicker? They don't even realize it. They honestly think they're doing a stellar job "managing" you when, in reality, they're the human equivalent of a malfunctioning Roomba, running around in circles, crashing into walls, and making everything worse.

Unraveling Workplace Chaos Caused by Toxic Managers

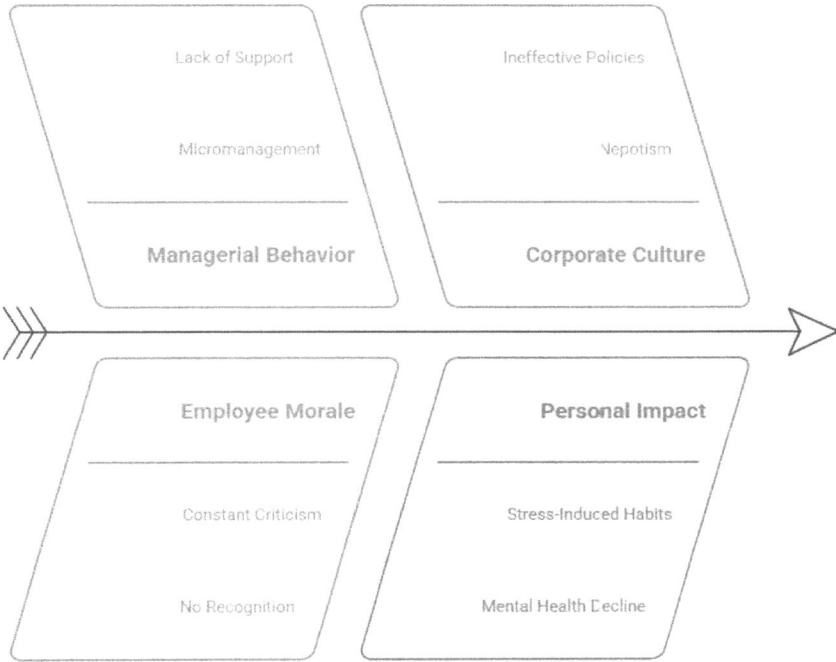

Lack of Support

Ineffective Policies

Micromanagement

Nepotism

Managerial Behavior

Corporate Culture

Employee Morale

Personal Impact

Constant Criticism

Stress-Induced Habits

No Recognition

Mental Health Decline

Let's Talk About Sarah

Let me introduce you to Sarah. Sarah, like you, was once a bright - eyed, hopeful employee. She had dreams. She had ambitions. But then she encountered her MF—a boss whose sole purpose in life seemed to be making her feel like a piece of gum stuck to the bottom of a corporate loafer. Every day, without fail, this boss would go on some kind of ridiculous power trip, finding new and exciting ways to make Sarah question all her life choices. How did Sarah cope? With donuts, of course. Because why waste money on therapy when you can eat your feelings in the form of sugary, fried dough?

But Sarah didn't just eat donuts for the sugar high—although, let's be real, donuts *do* help. No, she was mainlining those little circles of happiness because her job was slowly consuming her soul, and donuts were the only thing that numbed the pain. Before she knew it, she'd gained 15 pounds and was experiencing a mental breakdown every time she walked by a bakery. Her job wasn't just destroying her spirit, it was affecting her waistline—and, let's face it, nobody should have to choose between sanity and skinny jeans.

But here's where things really go south: Sarah wasn't just stressed at work. Oh no, her MF had effectively implanted a stress - inducing microchip in her brain that followed her everywhere. Weekends? Ruined. Holidays? A joke. Vacations? Hilarious. Because you don't really "escape" when you work for an MF. They live rent - free in your head, 24/7, making you wake up in a cold sweat thinking about that one email you forgot to send three weeks ago. You're basically trapped in a never - ending episode of *Survivor*, except instead of winning a million dollars, you win another week of passive - aggressive Slack messages and micromanagement[3].

And don't even get me started on the anxiety. Oh, the anxiety. It's like that constant hum of dread that follows you around, whispering in your ear, "You're not good enough. You're about to be found out. Everyone is watching you, and they all know you're a fraud." It's the kind of anxiety that makes you want to scream into a pillow, but instead, you just smile and nod through another pointless team - building exercise while you slowly die inside.

Ah, Promotions...or Lack Thereof

Ah, the sweet, sweet promise of a promotion—the holy grail of the corporate world. Except, oops! You've been passed over for the third time, and your MF is still feeding you the same line of "just keep doing what you're doing, and eventually, you'll get there." Spoiler alert: you won't. You're stuck

---

[3] Horrible Bosses: Are American Workers Quitting Their Jobs or Quitting Their Managers?

in a never - ending loop of rejection, like some sort of Sisyphean torture, except instead of rolling a boulder uphill, you're rolling your hopes and dreams straight into the trash can.

Who needs a promotion though, when you can be the trusty sidekick to your MF's half - baked leadership? It's like being Robin to their Batman, except instead of saving Gotham, you're just saving them from their own incompetence. And guess what? You'll get exactly zero credit for it. While you're not - so - bright coworkers are racking up promotions, bonuses, and praise, you'll be sitting in the corner, sipping your tenth cup of coffee, and wondering how your life became a scene from *Office Space*.

And what about the lost pay raises that should have come with those promotions? Oh, don't even get me started. Let's talk about the years of under compensation you've endured. While the nephew of your MF is zooming by in his new sports car, thanks to his *fabulous* new promotion, you're stuck checking your bank balance, wondering how you're still being paid like an intern while doing twice the work of your "promoted" colleagues. Those phantom pay raises are just one more notch in the belt of corporate cruelty. You worked those long hours, skipped those vacations, and for what? To stay stuck in the same financial purgatory you've been in since your entry - level days.

But don't despair, I've got some snarky survival tips for you. Grab your sad little coffee mug, slap on your best "I'm totally fine" face, and let's dive into how you can handle being overlooked for the 857th time.

Case in point—Mike. Poor Mike. Mike had been promised a promotion for five long years. Five years of missed birthdays, late nights, and canceled weekends. And what did he get? Nothing. Zero. Zilch. Because his MF decided to give the promotion to their nephew, whose only qualification was being able to share a last name. That's right, nepotism strikes again! And to add insult to that injury, those five years of lost pay raises have disappeared into the ether. The bonuses, the extra vacation days, the salary bumps—all gone. It's like watching your paycheck get a lobotomy.

But Mike didn't take it lying down. Oh no, Mike did the only thing you can do in that situation—he quit. Packed up his desk, marched out, and never looked back. And let me tell you, there's nothing more satisfying than watching your MF's face when you hand in your resignation. It's like watching someone realize their favorite toy is being taken away.

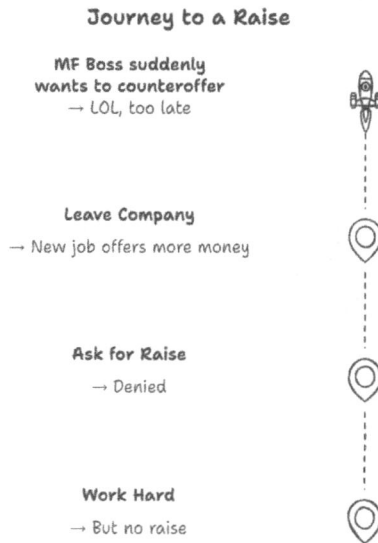

Journey to a Raise

MF Boss suddenly wants to counteroffer
→ LOL, too late

Leave Company
→ New job offers more money

Ask for Raise
→ Denied

Work Hard
→ But no raise

The Great Turnover Game - A Corporate Reality Show

And let's not forget the turnover problem—the ultimate game of corporate musical chairs where the only prize is getting the hell out of dodge. Everyone's bailing, and your company is hemorrhaging money faster than your MF can say "synergy." And what does the company do? Nothing. They sit back and wonder why half the workforce has decided to leave while promoting the same toxic MFs to higher positions. It's like they're collecting terrible managers like Pokémon cards, trying to see how many they can gather before the whole company collapses.

Fun fact: Did you know that 63% of people leave their jobs because of bad managers?[4] Yeah, half of the workforce is out the door because of people like your MF. And what does your company do in response? Hire someone new, spend six months training them, and hope they don't realize they've walked into a dumpster fire before they too, hit the eject button. It's like watching a never - ending episode of *The Office*, except there's no Jim, no Pam, and no happy ending.

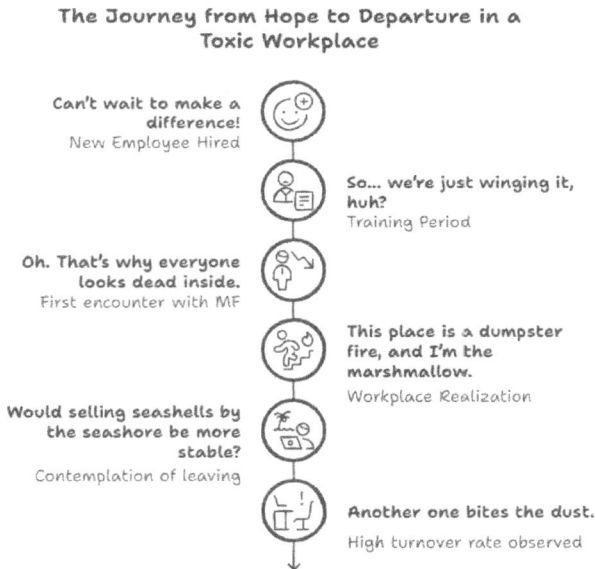

The Journey from Hope to Departure in a Toxic Workplace

Can't wait to make a difference!
New Employee Hired

So... we're just winging it, huh?
Training Period

Oh. That's why everyone looks dead inside.
First encounter with MF

This place is a dumpster fire, and I'm the marshmallow.
Workplace Realization

Would selling seashells by the seashore be more stable?
Contemplation of leaving

Another one bites the dust.
High turnover rate observed

But hey, why bother addressing the real problem? Let's just keep promoting these MFs, losing money, and pretending like everything's fine.

---

4   https://trainingindustry.com/magazine/jul-aug-2020/measuring-the-impact-of-a-bad-boss/#:~:text=When%20it%20comes%20to%20our,of%20%2475%2C000%20per%20direct%20report

Sounds like a solid business strategy, right? Or maybe they're just too chicken to make a change. Too afraid of stirring up the status quo. After all, who's got the guts to fire a Middle - Finger when it's easier to just let them run the show while pretending it's not a complete disaster?

MFs: The Grandmasters of Procrastination

MFs, they're like the grandmasters of procrastination! They might deliver impressive results for a while, but in the long run, they're like a party balloon filled with too much air—just waiting to pop! They really know how to turn up the heat on their employees, leading to a revolving door of staff and productivity that's as low as a limbo stick! It's as if they're in a competition for the title of "Most Miserable Person," and they're taking it way too seriously!

But here's the kicker: folks can only handle being treated like a doormat for just so long before they start looking for a new welcome mat! Eventually, they'll be off searching for a place where their thoughts and feelings are treated like royalty, rather than being tossed aside like last week's leftovers! And when they finally decide to make their grand exit, you'll be left in a hilarious game of musical chairs, desperately searching for a new partner in crime! I must say, it is akin to attempting to balance flaming swords while riding a unicycle on a tightrope. Oh boy! Wharton Professor Matthew Bidwell suggests that it might take a new employee a whopping two years to finally figure out where the coffee machine is and how to use the printer without causing a paper jam! That's like, an eternity wrapped in a burrito of time! Time that you could be using to, I don't know, actually keep your business from turning into a circus.

So, what's the deal with companies holding onto those not - so - great bosses? Are they collecting them like trading cards or something? It's not like they're living under a rock or anything! They must be aware that their employees are making a grand exit, like it's a mass exodus or something! But maybe they're just too chicken to take any action! Perhaps they're just too scared to make a splash! Or maybe they're just too occupied with their cash counting competition to notice anything else!

That being said, it goes beyond financial gain. It's all about the folks, isn't it? It's all about crafting a workplace that's actually fun and not a snooze fest! Where folks are treated like the treasures they are, and high - fives are handed out like candy! Where they can show up to work without the fear of their sanity taking a permanent vacation.

The Bottom Line

So, here's the deal—you're not crazy. You're not weak. And you're definitely not the problem. Your MF is. You don't have to keep sacrificing your mental health, your weekends, or your wardrobe (seriously, donuts are hard on pants) for a job that treats you like a disposable office supply. You deserve better than what you're dealing with, and the best part is—you hold the power to walk away.

And if you're wondering, "What about my MF? Will they miss me?" Probably not. They'll just move on to their next victim, but you'll finally be free. It's like a permanent vacation from the madness—and who doesn't want that?

Example from Personal Experience

It started, as most terrible ideas do, with an email.

Subject: NEW REQUIREMENT - Weekly Student Engagement Reports

I sighed before I even opened it. The body of the message confirmed my suspicions:

"Dear Educators, in our continued effort to improve student outcomes, all teachers will now be required to submit a "weekly engagement report" detailing each student's level of participation. This will help us track disengaged learners and provide necessary interventions. Your cooperation is appreciated."

I stared at the screen, the weight of the absurdity settling in. I had 140 students across multiple classes. I barely had time to grade their assignments, let alone analyze their weekly enthusiasm levels like some kind of academic sports commentator.

How, exactly, was I supposed to quantify engagement? Was I meant to rank their commitment on a scale from "eager hand - raiser" to "stares into the abyss"? Should I assign a point system? Five points for asking a thoughtful question, two points for nodding at the right moment, and a negative ten for audibly sighing when I announce group work.

At my next staff meeting, the administrator in charge of this new initiative addressed our unspoken resistance.

"This is just about accountability," they assured us. "We need to know who's engaged and who's falling through the cracks."

I raised a hand. "So, to clarify, you want a written, individualized assessment of engagement levels for every student every week?"

A nod.

I pressed on. "And will we be provided with additional time to complete this? Maybe a student - free planning period or reduced admin work to compensate for the added load?"

The administrator chuckled as if I'd suggested recess for teachers. "We know you all manage your time well. This should only take a few extra minutes per class."

I exchanged glances with my colleagues. A few extra minutes? That was six reports per student per month. 840 reports per semester. And I was just one teacher. Multiply that across the whole staff, and they'd have enough data on 'student engagement' to rival the NSA.

I tried a different approach. "What exactly happens if a student is marked as 'disengaged'?"

The administrator hesitated. "Well, we'll discuss potential interventions."

I raised an eyebrow. "So, we're doing all this extra paperwork without a clear action plan for what to do with the data?"

More hesitation. "Well... the data itself is valuable."

I leaned back, crossing my arms. "For who?"

Silence.

By Friday, I had a system. Instead of agonizing over detailed reports, I typed up a generic comment bank:

"Student is actively engaged and participates regularly."

"Student is quietly engaged but does not often volunteer responses."

"Student appears disengaged at times but completes work."

"Student struggles with focus and participation."

Then I *randomly* assigned them.

Because if they were going to waste her time, I was going to waste theirs right back.

Chapter 03:
Identifying Red Flags Early

Ah, the elusive quest for the perfect job—like searching for a unicorn in a field of donkeys. You think you've struck gold, but it turns out to be just another mirage in the vast wasteland of corporate gloom. For instance, getting a gig at a company that boasts a lively and colorful office vibe might look like a dream come true, but when you dig a little deeper, you find out that work - life balance is just a myth, and employees are clocking in marathon hours without so much as a thank you or a snack break! Or worse, they're clocking in for massive hours' worth of pay, attempting to look busy, but spend their day trying to get the high score on Candy Crush. You came to work and contribute to a company you believe in and they came for play time. In the end, landing the perfect job isn't just about the shiny perks and benefits that catch your eye; it's really about finding a company that actually cares about your well - being and helps you grow as a person. Who knew job hunting could be so deep, right?

First up, we have the infamous "mandatory fun" days. You know the ones—those cheerful little gatherings where you're forced to engage in team - building exercises that make you want to gouge your eyes out with a spoon. Nothing says "we value your time" quite like a day spent playing trust - falls with people you barely know while your actual work piles up like dirty laundry. If your boss is more excited about organizing a scavenger hunt than about meeting quarterly goals, you might want to start looking for the nearest exit. Because let's be real: if they're prioritizing "fun" over productivity, you're in for a wild ride on the express train to Burnout City.

Then there are the bosses who love meetings more than results. You know the type—those who schedule a meeting to discuss the next meeting, which will, of course, lead to yet another meeting. It's like a never - ending cycle of corporate purgatory. If you find yourself spending more time in meetings than actually doing your job, congratulations! You've stumbled into a toxic workplace where the only thing getting accomplished is the art of wasting time. And let's not forget the classic "let's circle back" phrase, which is just corporate speak for "I have no idea what I'm doing, but I'm going to pretend I do."

Now, let's talk about the culture of appearances. In a toxic workplace, it's all about looking busy rather than actually being productive. You'll notice that the office is filled with people who are more concerned with their image than their output. If your coworkers are more focused on perfecting their LinkedIn profiles than on delivering results, you might want to take a step back and reassess your life choices. Because when the culture values appearances over actual work, you're likely to find yourself in a never - ending cycle of backstabbing and office politics.

And let's not forget the classic sign of a toxic workplace: the revolving door of employees. If you notice that your department has a turnover rate that rivals a fast - food restaurant, it's time to raise an eyebrow. Chloe thought she had hit the jackpot when she landed her new job, only to discover that her department had a turnover rate of 300%. That's right— 300%. It's like a game of musical chairs, except the music never stops, and you're left standing alone in the corner, wondering what went wrong. Spoiler alert: it's not you, it's the toxic environment that's driving everyone away.[5]

---

[5] Neaves, E. (2017). It's Not You, It's Me: An Inductive Exploration of Employee Accounts for Quitting.

High employee turnover

Pros 〈vs〉 Cons

Pros		Cons	
Frequent new hires		Toxic work environment	
Fresh perspectives		Low morale	
		Constant training	
		Loss of experienced staff	
		Increased recruitment costs	

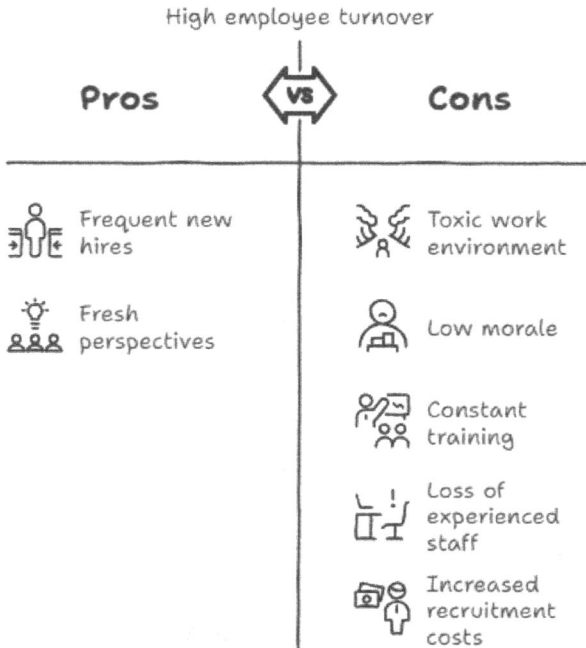

Chloe learned this the hard way. She was lured in by the promise of a ping - pong table and "mandatory fun" days, thinking she had found her dream job. But as she watched her coworkers flee faster than rats from a sinking ship, she realized that no amount of foosball could make up for the lack of respect and clear leadership. It's like putting a fresh coat of paint on a crumbling building—no matter how pretty it looks on the outside, the foundation is still a disaster waiting to happen.

So, what can you do to spot these red flags before it's too late? Well, for starters, pay attention to the vibe in the office. If the atmosphere feels more like a pressure cooker than a collaborative space, it's time to take a step back. Trust your gut—if something feels off, it probably is. And don't ignore the signs just because you're desperate for a job. Remember, it's better to be unemployed than to be stuck in a toxic environment that drains your soul.

The fine art of spotting a Middle - Finger Manager (MF) before you're trapped in a corporate nightmare. It's like trying to find a needle in a haystack, except the haystack is on fire and the needle is a ticking time bomb. Let's break down how to decode job descriptions and interview language to avoid future disasters.

How to identify a toxic workplace?

Office Vibe
A pressure cooker atmosphere indicates a toxic environment.

Management Style
Vague promises from management suggest potential micromanagement.

Employee Turnover
High turnover rates signal a toxic workplace.

Job Description
Buzzwords may indicate unrealistic expectations.

- **Job Descriptions**: Beware of the buzzwords! If you see phrases like "dynamic team environment" or "fast - paced culture," it's a signal to proceed with caution. These often translate to "we expect you to work yourself to the bone while we pretend to care about your well - being." And "opportunity for growth"? More like "You'll be stuck doing the same mind - numbing tasks forever, but at least you'll be busy!"

- **Interview Red Flags**: During the interview, pay attention to how your potential boss discusses the team. If they rave about the "family - like atmosphere" and "office perks" instead of the actual job responsibilities, it's a major warning sign[6]. Sure, pizza parties and ping - pong tables sound fun, but if that's the highlight, you might be signing up for a reality show rather than a career. Just ask Tim, who was drawn in by the promise of a "family" that turned out to be more like a cult. He ended up working 60 - hour weeks because his "family" expected him to "pitch in" after hours—for free. Spoiler alert: Tim's family didn't even send him a birthday card.

- **Vague Expectations**: Watch out for vague language when discussing job expectations. If your potential boss can't clearly articulate what success looks like, it's time to run. Phrases like "we're looking for someone who can hit the ground running" or "we value initiative" are just code for "we have no idea what we want, but we expect you to figure it out." It's like being handed a map with no destination—good luck with that!

- **Management Style**: When asked about their management style, if the answer is something like "I like to empower my team" or "I believe in open communication," take it with a grain of salt. These are often the same people who will micromanage you into oblivion while pretending they're giving you the freedom to thrive. It's like being offered a cookie while they hold the jar just out of reach.

- **Asking the Right Questions:** To get through this danger safely, you need to ask the right questions. Don't just nod your head, probe further down. Find out how often people leave the team, how they measure progress, and what a normal workweek looks like. You've done well if they start to sweat or dodge. You just found a possible MF in its natural environment.

People who are trying to find their way in the modern workplace need to be able to spot the red flags in business culture. These not - so - subtle

---

[6] Koonce, R. (1997). Spotting red flags in a job interview. *Training & Development, 51*(2), 15-16.

hints can often show that a job that seems like a dream could be a trash fire waiting to happen. One of the most glaring indicators is high turnover rates. If employees are constantly leaving, it's a clear sign that something is fundamentally wrong, whether it's poor management, unrealistic expectations, or a toxic environment that drives people away.

Think about it, if you walked into a restaurant and saw a bunch of people running out the door, you'd probably think twice before sitting down for a meal. The same logic applies to a company with a revolving door. It's not just about the employees who are leaving; it's about the ones who are staying behind. Are they just waiting for their chance to escape, or are they actually happy to be there? If it's the former, you might want to reconsider your job offer.

Unclear expectations are another significant red flag.[7] When job roles and responsibilities are vague, it creates confusion and frustration among employees. If management frequently shifts goals or fails to articulate what success looks like, it leads to a chaotic atmosphere that can sap motivation and productivity. Employees need clarity to thrive, and a lack of it can be detrimental. Imagine being told to build a house without a blueprint or instructions. You'd probably end up with a wonky structure that's more likely to collapse than stand the test of time.

The disconnect between a company's stated values and its actual practices is perhaps the most disheartening sign of all. A mission statement that sounds impressive but is not reflected in daily operations reveals a level of hypocrisy that can be demoralizing. For instance, when Lisa joined her new company, she was excited to see the mission statement prominently displayed on every wall. However, as she observed the day - to - day operations, it became painfully clear that those values were merely for show.

---

[7] Pope, B., Siegman, A. W., Blass, T., & Cheek, J. (1972). Some effects of discrepant role expectations on interviewee verbal behavior in the initial interview. *Journal of Consulting and Clinical Psychology, 39*(3), 501.

The reality was far from the ideal, and she quickly realized that her "dream job" was more akin to a bad reality show.

It's like when a friend tells you they're a great cook, but when you come over for dinner, they serve you a frozen pizza. You start to wonder if they're just full of hot air. The same thing happens when a company claims to value innovation but punishes risk - taking. It's like they're saying, "Hey, we want you to think outside the box, but only if it's a box we've approved." It's a recipe for disaster, and it's a clear sign that the company is more interested in looking good than actually being good.

Another red flag is when a company is more concerned with appearances than actual results. If they're spending more time and money on fancy marketing campaigns than on actual product development, it's a sign that they're more interested in looking successful than actually being successful. It's like when someone spends all their time taking selfies but never actually leaves the house. They might look great on social media, but in reality, they're not actually doing anything.

And then there's the issue of accountability[8]. If a company is not willing to take responsibility for its mistakes, it's a sign that they're not interested in growth or improvement. It's like when a friend always blames someone else for their problems. You start to wonder if they're ever going to take ownership of their actions. The same thing happens when a company is always shifting the blame to someone else. It's a sign that they're not interested in learning from their mistakes, and that's a recipe for disaster.

These experiences serve as an aide - mémoire: if a job sounds too good to be true, it probably is. The warning signs are often there, waiting to be noticed. It's like when you're on a date, and the other person seems too perfect. You start to wonder if they're hiding something. The same thing

---

[8] Gordon, R. A., Rozelle, R. M., & Baxter, J. C. (1988). The effect of applicant age, job level, and accountability on the evaluation of job applicants. *Organizational Behavior and Human Decision Processes, 41*(1), 20-33.

happens when a company seems too good to be true. They might be hiding something, and it's up to you to do your research and find out what it is.

So, what can you do to avoid falling into the trap of a toxic workplace? First, do your research. Look up reviews from current and former employees. Check out the company's social media accounts to see what they're really like. And don't be afraid to ask tough questions during the interview process. If they seem evasive or secretive, it's a sign that they might be hiding something.

Second, trust your instincts. If something feels off, it probably is. Don't ignore your gut feeling just because the company seems perfect on paper. Remember, if it sounds too good to be true, it probably is.

Finally, don't be afraid to walk away. If you realize that the company is not what you thought it was, it's okay to leave. It's better to cut your losses early than to stick around and hope that things will get better. Remember, you deserve to work in a place that values and respects you, and if that's not happening, it's time to move on.

Really, if you want to make it in the modern workplace, you need to be able to spot the red flags in company culture. It's not always easy, but it's worth it in the end. So, the next time you're considering a new job, remember to keep your eyes open and your wits about you. It might just save you from a world of trouble.

Chapter 04:
Surviving the Workplace Warzone

Welcome to the battlefield known as the workplace, where the coffee is lukewarm, the deadlines are tighter than your MFs grip on the last donut, and your colleagues believe they're the reincarnation of Einstein—despite their last brilliant idea being to swap the office chairs for yoga balls. Good luck with that! Getting through this warzone takes more than just a strong cup of coffee; it calls for a whole toolkit of survival tactics! So, get ready, because we're plunging into the fine craft of avoiding bullets—both the figurative kind and, let's face it, occasionally the real deal (yes, I'm talking about you, stapler - launching Steve).

First things first: let's chat about those folks who strut around like they've got all the answers, but in reality, they couldn't find the right end of a spoon! You totally know the kind, right? They waltz into the office as if they're the kings and queens of the corporate jungle, brandishing a PowerPoint presentation so dull it could lull a caffeinated squirrel into a deep slumber. They're absolutely certain their route is the only one that matters, even when the GPS is practically waving a flag saying, "Wrong way, buddy!"

Now, take this same energy and apply it to the wonderful world of MFs. These are the folks who live, breathe, and probably dream in email format. They send messages at 5:02 PM on a Friday and expect a response by 5:03 PM. But when it comes to actually answering an email that requires leadership, guidance, or, god forbid, decision - making? Suddenly, they vanish like a magician's assistant in a cheap Vegas act.

Ever sent an email about a critical classroom issue? Maybe your classroom heater is stuck on a 'volcano,' or little Timmy discovered his calling as a WWE wrestler mid - lesson, and you need support. How does your MFA respond? They don't. They never do. However, accidentally miss checking the "Mandatory Faculty Wellness Survey" they sent at 7:15 AM on a Saturday.

"Please see me in my office at your earliest convenience."

One instance was when I sent five separate emails about a kid who left her classroom every day and never came back (seriously, I thought he had built an underground tunnel system).

No response. Nothing. Crickets.

But when I accidentally missed a "motivational" email about teamwork from the same MF?

"Let's schedule a check - in to discuss professional accountability."

Apparently, my failure to acknowledge the email equivalent of a Pinterest quote was a larger crisis than the student slowly morphing into Houdini during the third period.

Coping Strategies

Navigating Workplace Challenges with Style

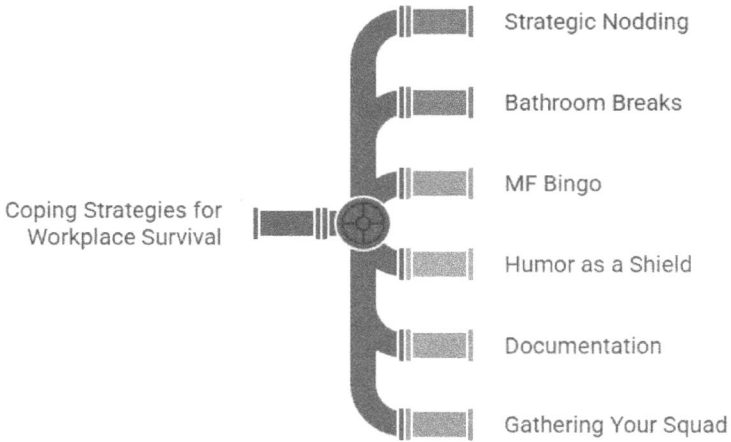

Coping Strategies for Workplace Survival

Strategic Nodding

Bathroom Breaks

MF Bingo

Humor as a Shield

Documentation

Gathering Your Squad

1. **Master the Art of Strategic Nodding:** When your MF is rambling on about their latest "brilliant" idea (which, let's be real, is just a rehash of last week's disaster), perfect the art of nodding. Nod, like you're in a yoga class, but keep your eyes glazed over like you're staring into the abyss. This way, you can mentally check out while still appearing engaged. Bonus points if you can throw in an occasional "That's interesting!" or "Great point!" to keep them feeling validated. Just remember, it's all about survival, not sincerity.

2. **Schedule "Bathroom Breaks" During Meetings:** I interviewed Kelly, a disgruntled worker, about this very issue. She discovered that the best way to cope with her MF's endless, pointless meetings was to schedule "bathroom breaks" at strategic intervals. It's a timeless trick that lets you slip away from the chaos without anyone batting an eye. Just make sure to time it perfectly—like when your buddy starts rambling about the shade of the new office paint. Believe me,

your future self will be sending you thank - you notes when you're not trapped in a 20 - minute saga about "the psychological effects of beige."

3. **Create a "MF Bingo" Card:** Turn your daily grind into a game! Create a bingo card filled with your MF's favorite phrases, like "synergy," "circle back," and "let's take this offline." Every time they say one of these gems, mark it off. When you get a bingo, treat yourself to a snack or a mini dance party in your cubicle. It's a fun way to cope with the absurdity of it all while keeping your spirit high. Just be careful not to get too loud—no one wants to explain to HR why you were caught doing the Macarena at your desk.

4. **Use Humor as Your Shield:** When all else fails, humor is your best defense. Discover methods to chuckle at the absurdity of your circumstances. Swap your epic tales of workplace battles with coworkers over lunch and transform your collective struggles into a hilarious stand - up act. You'll connect over the ridiculousness of it all, and chuckles are a fantastic way to let off some steam. Just keep it breezy—nobody wants to be the office chatterbox, but a sprinkle of playful teasing never did any harm!

5. **Document Everything:** If your MF is always wrong, it's essential to keep a record of their blunders. Document meetings, decisions, and any questionable directives. This isn't just for your sanity; it's also a safety net. If things go south, you'll have evidence to back you up. Plus, it gives you a sense of control in a chaotic environment. Just make sure to keep it discreet - no one wants to be caught with an "MF Blunders" folder on their desktop.

6. **Gather Your Squad:** In a battlefield, having your backup crew is a total game changer! Find your fellow warriors—those colleagues who totally understand your struggles and can lend a listening ear when you need it most. Create a "survivor's club" where you can let

off steam, swap survival tips, and maybe even brainstorm your great escape (figuratively speaking, of course). Having a crew of folks who think like you can turn the daily slog into a bit of a laugh fest!

7. **Practice the Art of Selective Listening:** Sometimes, you just have to tune out the noise. When your buddy starts rambling about their weekend escapades or the latest office drama, just tune in and out like a pro! Zero in on the crucial bits and let everything else drift by like a catchy tune you can't quite remember the words too. It's a talent that requires some serious honing, but once you nail it, you'll be strutting around like a stress - free peacock!

8. **Plan Your Exit Strategy:** If the workplace warzone becomes too much to handle, it's essential to have an exit strategy. Whether it's updating your resume, networking, or casually browsing job boards, having a plan in place can give you a sense of control. Remember, you're not a prisoner in this war zone; you have options. Just like in a video game, sometimes the best strategy is to find the nearest exit and make a run for it.

Protecting Your Work

Ah, the classic showdown of claiming your well - deserved glory! It's like attempting to snag the final slice of pizza at a party—everyone's staring at it, and if you don't move quickly, some MF will swoop in and snatch it right out from under you. You've put your blood, sweat, and tears into that project, and the last thing you need is for some oblivious goofball to stroll in and soak up the spotlight of your genius. So, what's the secret sauce for safeguarding your genius and making sure everyone knows you're the mastermind behind it all? Let's plunge into some strategies that go from sneaky to hilariously bold.

This is your first line of defense. Make sure to jot down every brilliant idea, contribution, and chat about your projects—because who doesn't love a good trip down memory lane, right? Imagine it as your very own "Look what I did!" album. Whether it's emails, meeting notes, or even a good old - fashioned notebook, having a paper trail can save your bacon when the sneaky folks try to pull a fast one on you. If they try to claim your work, you can whip out your documentation like a superhero revealing their secret identity. "Surprise! It's me, the real genius behind this masterpiece!"

When you're knee - deep in a project, don't forget to spill the beans about your brilliant ideas and how far you've come with your crew and those MFs. Keep those updates rolling in, and don't hold back on sharing your brilliant thoughts! This way, it's clear who's behind the wheel of this crazy ride! If your MF decides to play the credit game later, just give them a friendly nudge about all those emails you fired off like confetti! "Oh, you mean the project I elaborated on in my five thrilling updates last week?" Oh, absolutely, that was totally me!

Think twice before you let loose your brilliant thoughts into the wild! If you're tossing around ideas in a meeting, don't be shy—let your voice be heard and show off those brilliant thoughts of yours! If you're fretting over someone swiping your brilliant ideas, why not present them in a way that screams, "I'm the genius behind this!" Instead of saying, "What if we do this?" how about, "I've been mulling over this idea, and here's my grand vision for how it could all play out!" This way, you're not just tossing ideas into the abyss; you're staking your claim like a pirate on a treasure map!

When it comes to emails, the "reply all" button can be like a trusty sidekick or a mischievous villain lurking in the shadows. If your MF thinks they can snag the spotlight for your hard work in a group email, don't hold back—hit that button and let the truth shine through! A perfectly timed "reply all" can turn into a spectacular spectacle of public embarrassment. "Thanks for the kind words, but just to clarify, I was the one who developed that strategy. Thrilled to spill the beans! It's like launching a surprise party in the middle of a snooze - fest—out of nowhere, everyone's wide awake!

In the chaotic battlefield of the office, it's extremely important to position yourself as the ultimate guru in your field of knowledge. Whether it's through presentations, sharing insights in meetings, or even casual chit - chat, ensure that folks link your name with your work like peanut butter and jelly! When your MF tries to take credit, others will be quick to point out that it was you who came up with the idea. "Wait, wasn't that Kelly's brainchild? I remember her talking about it last week!"

Scout out some coworkers who can back up your awesomeness at work! If you've got coworkers who actually notice your brilliance, they can totally turn up the volume on your praise when it's time for a little recognition party! It's like assembling a quirky squad of cheerleaders ready to jump in when the MFs try to pull a sneaky move. "Oh, you really believed that was your brainchild? Hilarious, because I can totally picture Kelly showcasing that idea at our last meeting!"

Sometimes, you've got to channel your inner daredevil to keep your masterpiece safe! If you think your brilliant ideas are getting lost in the shuffle, don't hesitate to raise your voice and let the world know you're here! "Hey, I just wanted to make sure everyone knows I was the one who put together that report. I'd love to hear your thoughts on it!" It's all about strutting your stuff and ensuring your hard work doesn't slip through the cracks like a banana peel!

If you're stuck in a workplace where your brilliant ideas are being swiped like snacks at a party, it might be time to think about making a grand exit! Everyone deserves to be in a situation where their contributions are celebrated, not tossed aside like last week's leftovers! Sometimes, the best way to guard your genius is to scout out a fresh arena where your skills will be celebrated and adored.

Real - Life Example

I interviewed Kelly, a disgruntled worker, about this very issue. She recounted a moment when her manager tried to snag the spotlight for her work. In a perfectly timed "reply all" email, Kelly made it clear who the true genius of the project was. Mic drop! She whipped up her message with the finesse of a chef, making sure it was as sharp as a tack and dressed to impress! "Thanks for the shout - out, but just to set the record straight, I was the mastermind behind the initial concept and the one who actually made it happen. Thrilled to chat more about it!" The email zipped through the office like a gossip train, and before you knew it, everyone was suddenly in the know about who really deserved the spotlight. Sometimes, a little public shaming can really spice things up, and Kelly's daring stunt not only snatched her work back but also opened the floodgates for others to channel their inner warriors and fight for themselves. In the office battlefield, it's all about timing your comebacks and delivering them with style!

~⌀

Chapter 05:
Fighting Back: Legal and Professional Options

Fighting Back: Legal and Professional Options

Introduce yourself to the legendary clash of workplace rights, where the stakes are through the roof. In this part of the book, we're dipping headfirst into the occasionally murky waters of legal and professional options available to you when your workplace turns into a chaotic circus of toxic shenanigans. Spoiler alert: it's not merely about dodging airborne staplers and those oh - so - subtle emails; it's about being savvy enough to know your rights and how to throw down when the MFs decide to overstep their bounds.

Wading through the wild waters of a toxic workplace can feel like an extreme sport, but don't worry, you've got a whole toolbox of legal and professional tricks up your sleeve! It's super important to load up on knowledge and resources to tackle any shenanigans or unfairness that might come your way! Don't just aim to dodge the madness; make sure you're waving your flag and giving that "World's Okayest Boss" a run for their money when they think they can boss you around! Keep your brain buzzing, stay in the loop, and be all set to spring into action when the moment strikes! You totally got this! Like a cat with nine lives, but way more confident!

Understanding Your Rights:

Let's be factual: figuring out workplace rights is like attempting to decipher a legal scroll from the time of the dinosaurs. But don't panic! We're here to simplify it so clearly that even your pet goldfish could get it—if only they could focus for a second! This part is your witty roadmap to determining whether your boss's latest command is genuinely against the law or just another typical Tuesday in the world of a bewildered genius.

First off, let's look into the hilariously ridiculous antics that toxic bosses often pull off. Oh, you know the kind! They believe they can just waltz in and ask for free overtime, throw shade at employees like it's a sport, or turn the office into a scene from a horror movie just because they spilled their coffee. Classic! It's as if they skipped the memo that the office isn't a set for a cringe - worthy reality show. So, how do you tell when their antics have gone from "irritating" to "breaking the law?"

Here's a little nugget of wisdom: if your boss is turning your work life into a bizarre reality show, it might be time to check out what rights you've got in this wild game. Are they really trying to get you to clock in some free labor? Are they giving you the cold shoulder because of your race, gender, or any other special badge you wear? If the answer is yes, well, look at you, superstar! You've just tripped over a possible legal oopsie - daisy!

But hey, no need to panic; you've got company in this epic showdown! Knowing your rights is like putting on your superhero cape against those sneaky MFs who believe they can pull a fast one! It's like carrying around a hidden bazooka—one that lets you declare, "Not today, buddy!"

I interviewed Carol, a disgruntled worker about this very issue. She recounted a time when her boss, in a fit of misguided authority, decided that everyone should work weekends without pay because "team spirit" was at an all - time low. Carol, feeling the weight of the world on her shoulders, didn't know her boss's behavior was illegal—until HR handed out a pamphlet that might as well have been titled, "Is Your Boss a Jerk?"

Armed with newfound knowledge (and a good lawyer), Carol decided to take action. She gathered her coworkers, and they collectively approached HR, armed with the pamphlet and a list of grievances that could rival a grocery list. "You know," she said, "I didn't realize that working for free was a thing. I thought we were all just volunteering for a really dysfunctional charity."

The HR rep, trying to suppress a laugh, explained the legal implications of their boss's demands. Carol and her coworkers learned that they had rights, and they weren't afraid to use them. They filed a formal complaint, and before long, their MF was called into a meeting that was less about "team spirit" and more about "you can't do that."

Legal Recourse

So, you've hit the hot and steamy moment! The coffee machine has thrown in the towel, your MF is hovering like a hawk, and you're ready to call it quits on this three - ring workplace extravaganza. It's time to get your legal game on, and we're here to help you navigate the process with a sprinkle of attitude! It's true that a little comedy may help reduce the tension of what's going to happen when it comes to taking serious action.

What to Do When You've Had Enough:

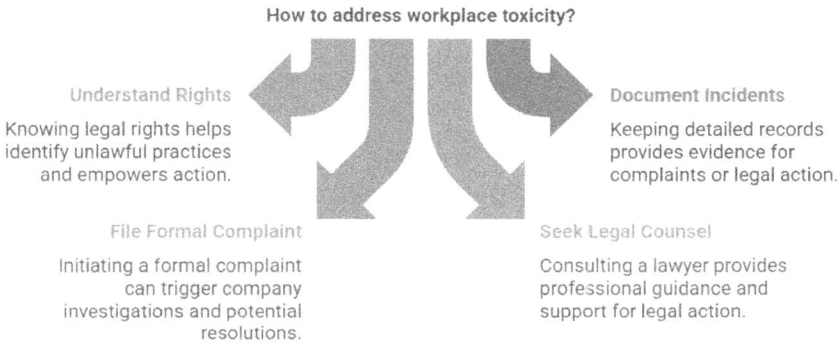

How to address workplace toxicity?

Understand Rights
Knowing legal rights helps identify unlawful practices and empowers action.

Document Incidents
Keeping detailed records provides evidence for complaints or legal action.

File Formal Complaint
Initiating a formal complaint can trigger company investigations and potential resolutions.

Seek Legal Counsel
Consulting a lawyer provides professional guidance and support for legal action.

Alright, let's get this party started: if you're thinking about taking the legal route, make sure you're documenting everything like it's the next big blockbuster hit! And I mean absolutely everything! Consider it your own little book of office shenanigans. Make sure to jot down all the juicy details—incidents, dates, times, and any poor souls who might have witnessed your MF shenanigans in action! This isn't just for your own sanity; it's your secret stash of fireworks for when you finally decide to throw a party of resistance!

Picture this: you're a detective in a crime drama, and your main foe is the villain. Plot twist, right? You can't just wing it; you need some solid proof to back up your claims! So, grab a pen and start collecting those eye - roll - inducing comments, the midnight emails begging for weekend work, and any moments of harassment that make you go, "Did that really just happen?" The fancier your notes, the more likely you'll impress someone—like a magician pulling a rabbit out of a hat, but with words instead! You want to create a masterpiece so striking that even a jury would be thinking, "Whoa, this person really needs a reality check!"

Once you've rounded up your evidence, it's showtime to file that formal complaint! This is where the fun really begins! You'll want to waltz right up to HR or the right department in your company like you own the place! And just a heads up, this isn't your typical coffee klatch; we're diving into some serious stuff here! You might want to perfect your "I'm totally serious right now" face in the mirror before you step in. Just don't crack a smile!

When you file that complaint, be clear and concise. Lay out the facts, and don't hold back. You're not there to make friends; you're there to make a point. If your MF has been acting like a tyrant, it's time to let HR know that you're not going to take it anymore.

Seeking Legal Counsel:

If HR is treating your complaint like a bad joke or if things are still a circus, it might be time to call in the legal clowns for backup. Oh boy, it's time to unleash the heavy artillery! Seek out a lawyer who knows employment law inside and out—ideally one with a reputation for being as fierce as a lioness defending her little ones. You need a savvy guide who can help you wade through the wild jungle of workplace rights and dodge those legal quicksand traps!

When you sit down with your lawyer, get ready to spill all the scandalous tea! This is your golden opportunity to dish out the juicy gossip on your MF and their hilarious shenanigans. Your lawyer will be your trusty sidekick, helping you navigate the wild world of legalese, whether it's haggling over a settlement or gearing up for an epic courtroom showdown. And don't fret; they'll make sure your sass stays fully charged while you tackle this adventure.

I interviewed Lisa, who had endured months of harassment from her MF. She described the moment she realized enough was enough. "I was sitting at my desk, and I thought, 'Why am I putting up with this nonsense?'" After documenting everything—every snide comment, every inappropriate email - Lisa decided it was time to take action.

She decided to take the plunge and filed a formal complaint with HR, but when that turned out to be as effective as a screen door on a submarine, she thought, "Why not consult a lawyer?" "I felt like I was finally grabbing the reins of my circus," she said. The grand finale? A deal that let her escape a nightmare job with a bonus for her troubles! "It was like hitting the jackpot, but instead of cash, I had a lawyer," she joked.

Lisa's tale is a hilarious reminder of the importance of having a backbone. When you've hit your limit, don't be shy about doing what it takes to stand up for yourself! After all, life's too short to let a total buzzkill mess with your work vibe. So, collect your proof, submit that complaint, and if it comes to it, get yourself a legal eagle! You totally got this! Like a cat with nine lives, but way more confident!

From "Frustrated" to "Formally Complaining:"

First things first: take a deep breath. You're not auditioning for a soap opera, so save the dramatic monologue about how your MF has wronged you for the stage! Instead, let's tackle this like a pro diplomat tiptoeing through a field of whoopee cushions. Here's the secret to transforming from a silent grumbler to a loud and proud voice without causing a ruckus!

Step 1: Informal Conversations with HR

Before you take the plunge into the deep end, maybe have a casual chit - chat with HR first! Imagine it as a casual coffee date—except, you know, without the coffee, since you probably don't want to unleash your caffeine - induced rants just yet. Set up a meeting and don't forget to bring your notes—unless you want to wing it and hope for the best! Present your case like a slick lawyer delivering a grand opening statement, not like a cranky employee airing their grievances after a long day at the office.

When you meet with HR, keep it professional. "I've noticed some concerning behaviors from my manager that I'd like to discuss" is a solid opener. Avoid phrases like "my boss is a total jerk" or "I can't stand this place." You're not there to air grievances; you're there to seek solutions.

Step 2: Document Everything

If your casual chit - chat doesn't spark any changes (and let's face it, it usually doesn't), it's time to level up your strategy! Write it all down, folks! Absolutely, I'm talking about the whole shebang! Make sure to jot down every little mishap, complete with dates, times, and all the juicy details of what went down. This isn't just for your peace of mind; it's your golden ticket when you choose to take things up a notch!

Imagine it as your own version of "War and Peace," but swap out the deep philosophical dilemmas for a delightful array of passive - aggressive emails. The fancier your documentation, the more impressive your case will look when you finally decide to strut your stuff to the next level.

Step 3: Formal Complaints

Now, if your MF continues to act like a tyrant, it's time to file a formal complaint. This is where you put on your big - kid pants and get serious. Write a clear and concise letter outlining your concerns, referencing your documentation, and stating what you hope to achieve.

When you submit your complaint, do it in a way that shows you mean business. "I'm formally requesting an investigation into the behavior of my manager, as it has created a hostile work environment." Boom! You've just leveled up from "frustrated employee" to "serious contender for workplace justice."

Step 4: Know When to Involve Legal Counsel

If everything else goes belly up and your MF is still causing chaos, it might just be time to think about calling in the lawyers! But before you get headfirst into a legal soap opera, have a chat with a lawyer who knows the ins and outs of employment law. They'll guide you through the next steps and make sure you're not dancing on any legal landmines.

I had a chat with Tim, who went from being a silent sufferer to launching a formal complaint after his boss decided to play hopscotch over all the boundaries. "I was just trying to do my job, but my buddy was making it a real circus," he said. What's Tim hiding in his mystery box? He documented everything as if he was gearing up for the most dramatic reality show reunion ever!

When he finally decided to take things up a notch, he managed to keep his composure like a pro. "I knew I had to waltz into HR like a pro, so I presented my case without turning into a total drama queen," he explained. Tim's meticulous strategy really hit the jackpot, and he managed to file a formal complaint that kicked off the whole circus of dealing with his MF's antics.

So, if you ever find yourself in a similar pickle, just keep in mind: you don't need to rocket from zero to sixty like a caffeinated squirrel on a sugar rush! Take your sweet time, jot down your wild adventures, and when things go sideways, raise an eyebrow with a mix of swagger and a sprinkle of caution! You totally got this! Go on, show the world what you're made of!

⤳

Chapter 06:
Navigating Career Moves and Transitions

Welcome back to the zany zoo of career moves and transitions, where safety is as elusive as a unicorn, so keep flipping those pages! Here, change is the only constant—and maybe a sprinkle of existential dread. Whether you're pondering a jump into a new job, a twist in your career path, or just trying to dodge the grasp of those MFs, this chapter is your trusty map. Think of it as your GPS for maneuvering the often - wild wilderness of workplace transitions, served with a side of chuckles to keep you from losing your marbles (or your lunch).

Planning Your Exit Strategy

Ah, the time has arrived to seize the day! You've weathered the storm, faced the drama, and tackled the daily shenanigans from your MFs, and now you're primed to utter those two magnificent words: "I quit." But before you go all out with a dramatic exit—like hurling your stapler at the wall and making a grand exit worthy of a reality TV star—you might want to take a moment to ponder a more calculated approach. After all, you don't want to set fire to every bridge in sight while you're making your great getaway!

When to Say "I Quit"

First things first: how do you know when it's time to pack up your desk and bid adieu to the madness? Look for the signs. If you find yourself daydreaming about life as a professional cat cuddler or plotting your escape like a character in a heist movie, it might be time to start planning your exit strategy.

Ask yourself: Is the stress of dealing with your MFs outweighing the benefits of staying? Are you losing sleep over the latest round of passive - aggressive emails? If the answer is yes, congratulations! You've just earned yourself a one - way ticket to "I Quit" Island.

How to Quit Without Burning Bridges

Now that you've decided to make your move let's talk about how to do it gracefully—or at least with a semblance of dignity. Here's the game plan:

1. **Give Notice Like a Pro:** When you're ready to quit, don't just drop the bomb in the middle of a team meeting. Give your boss a little nudge in the right direction! A two - week notice is the usual script, but if you want to be the star of your own show, why not extend the curtain call a bit longer if you can? This isn't just about being sweet; it's about parting with a smile!

2. **Keep It Classy:** When you hand in your resignation, keep it professional. "I've decided to pursue other opportunities" is a classic line that works every time. Avoid phrases like "I can't take another minute of your nonsense" or "I'm outta here because you're all MFs." Trust me, your future self will thank you.

3. **Exit Interview? More Like Exit Opportunity:** If your company conducts exit interviews, treat it as a chance to provide constructive feedback. You can say something like, "I think the workplace could benefit from a little less chaos and a little more teamwork." Just

remember to keep it diplomatic. You're not there to roast your MFs; you're there to leave with your head held high.

4. **Stay LinkedIn - tact:** Before you take off, don't forget to link up with your colleagues on LinkedIn or other professional networks! You never know when you might need a buddy or a helpful hint down the road! Plus, it's always a treat to have someone to share a laugh with about the MFs you've moved on from!

Steps to a Graceful Exit

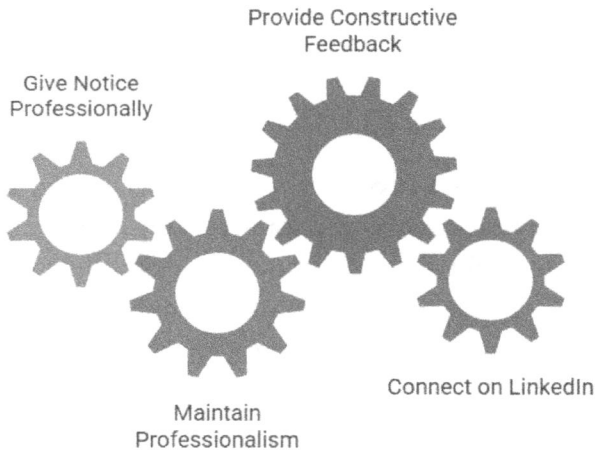

Provide Constructive
Feedback

Give Notice
Professionally

Connect on LinkedIn

Maintain
Professionalism

I had a chat with Mike, who managed to dodge the poison of a toxic workplace for years! After surviving the whirlwind of chaos and drama, he finally landed a new gig that didn't require him to dodge MFs on a daily basis. Talk about a job well done! But before he took his final bow, Mike ensured his new boss was fully in the loop about his departure. "I aimed to keep it real without coming off as a sour grape," he quipped.

When he handed in his resignation, he really knew how to exit with style! "I'm thrilled about this new opportunity, but I must say, the atmosphere here has been quite a tough nut to crack!" His boss was all ears for the feedback, and Mike waltzed out with his head held high and a reference that could light up a room!

So, as you gear up to steer your own career moves and transitions, keep in mind: it's all about plotting your getaway with a wink and a twirl of elegance. You can slip away from your MFs without leaving a path of pandemonium behind you. After all, you're not just tossing in the towel at a job; you're flipping the page to a new chapter of your career—ideally one that doesn't have you ducking staplers or dealing with the minefield of passive - aggressive emails.

Leveraging Experiences

Now, the trenches of a toxic workplace—where dreams take a permanent vacation and sanity is just a ghost of a chance! But have no fear! Just because you've wandered through the halls of MFs doesn't mean you can't transform those escapades into something worth its weight in gold! In fact, you can turn your time spent sidestepping drama into a goldmine of lessons learned (or, at the very least, a stash of side - splitting stories for your next job interview).

Let's be honest: if you've conquered a toxic workplace, you've probably honed skills that would make even the toughest gladiator green with envy! You've become a pro at wading through the wild waters of chaos, sidestepping those sneaky passive - aggressive remarks, and staying as cool as a cucumber while your MFs throw their little fits. So, how do you take those experiences and turn them into your next career "moo - ve"? Let's crack it open!

First, it's all about reshaping your story into a new frame of mind! Instead of seeing your time in the trenches as a string of misadventures, consider it a boot camp for bouncing back! You've mastered the art of juggling tough situations, chatting it up with finesse (even when your MFs are being a real handful), and keeping your chuckles intact when the going gets tough. These are skills that would make any employer's heart skip a beat!

Now, when it comes to job interviews, you want to highlight these experiences without turning them into a soap opera about office antics! Instead of saying, "I worked for a bunch of MFs who made my life miserable," try something like, "I had the pleasure of managing a uniquely challenging environment that really sharpened my skills in adaptability and conflict resolution." Bee - lieve it or not! You've just flipped a frown upside down, and you didn't even need to lift a finger!

And let's not overlook the tale - spinning magic. Everyone enjoys a tale that really knows how to leap over hurdles. When the topic of your last job comes up, don't just wing it—share a specific experience that really shows how you've soared to new heights! For instance, "In my previous position, I encountered some one - of - a - kind hurdles with management, which really drove me to sharpen my problem - solving skills." I picked up some skills to steer through tricky talks and champion myself and my crew!" Bang! Pow! You've just turned a frightful fable into a victorious yarn!

Let's proceed to chat about Lisa, who ditched her toxic job and didn't just survive—she really blossomed. When she strolled out the door, she carried a treasure trove of experiences that would leave anyone green with envy! Instead of wallowing in self - pity, Lisa decided to dig in and make the most of her time in the trenches. She flipped her worst job into the best thing that ever happened to her, all while wearing a grin and sharing a chuckle or two on the journey.

When Lisa hit the interview circuit, she didn't dodge the chance to chat about her history! Instead, she put it in the picture as a lesson to draw from. "I've mastered the art of juggling tricky personalities and dodging office drama," she would say, all while keeping a sparkle in her eye. Her interviewers were hooked, not just by her bounce - back ability but by her knack for cracking jokes amidst the mayhem.

So, as you get ready to spin your own yarn, keep in mind: it's all about reshaping your tale, sharing your saga with flair, and flaunting the talents you've picked up on your journey. You've been through the wash cycle, but that doesn't mean you can't spin your way to the other side with a grin on your face and a treasure trove of wisdom tucked away! After all, if you can outlast the MFs, you can tackle anything that crosses your path!

Framing Your Narrative

So, you've decided to cut ties with your toxic job, and now you're in a bit of a pickle trying to explain your exit to your next potential employer. You want to share your reasons for leaving without coming off like a jilted lover or a job - hungry puppy.

First things first: let's toss the frown and turn that upside down! You've dug deep with your MFs, and now it's time to turn that frown upside down and focus on the bright side! When asked why you left your last job, try to avoid turning it into a comedy show about your manager being a total train wreck. Instead, view it as a chance to flex your strengths and flaunt what you've picked up along the way!

For instance, rather than saying, "I left because my boss was a total nightmare," you might say, "I discovered that I flourish in workplaces that are more of a dream team!" Catch that clever twist, did you? You've just flipped a potential rant into a value - packed declaration about what you're seeking in your next gig!

Next, let's spin a yarn about the power of storytelling! Who doesn't enjoy a tale that really takes you on a journey of growth? It's like a plot twist in the book of life! When the topic of your last job comes up, don't just wing it—share a tale that really highlights your bounce - back ability! "While handling a tough work landscape, I discovered that teamwork and adaptability are the dynamic duo of success. I had to steer through some knotty situations, but it really helped me learn the ropes of effective communication and lend a hand to my colleagues!" Ta - da! You've just turned a fright fest into a victory lap, and you didn't even need to drop the MFs!

Now, let's take a peek at Kelly, who really hit the nail on the head with her next interview after dodging the grasp of middle - finger management. When asked why she left her last job, she didn't get caught up in the whirlwind or the theatrics. Instead, she zeroed in on the priceless nuggets of wisdom she picked up along the way. "I really bounced back with a lot of insight into resilience and the importance of teamwork," she said, all while sporting a grin that could lift spirits! Not once did she throw shade at her awful MFs, and her interviewers were left dazzled by her knack for shining a light on the positives.

Kelly's approach is a prime example of how to spin your tale effectively! By shining a light on your strengths and the lessons you've picked up along the way, you not only dodge the bitterness bullet but also set yourself up as a candidate who can tackle challenges with a touch of elegance.

So, as you get ready to spin the tale of your exit from that toxic job, keep in mind: it's all about crafting your story to highlight your growth and bounce - back ability! You've been through the wringer, but that doesn't mean you can't spin a yarn that leaves your next employer all wound up and eager to reel you in! After all, if you can dodge the MFs, you can flourish anywhere!

Chapter 07:
Hope for the Struggling Employee

If you're reading this, you're probably trapped in a work jungle, pondering how to endure another day filled with MFs, micromanagers, and meetings that could've easily been a quick email. You're likely feeling like you've stumbled into a wacky, never - ending dream where the coffee is bold, but your desire to keep going is even bolder. But hey, no need to panic, buddy; you're in good company! We've all experienced that classic moment, right? You know, the one where you end up with a t - shirt that's definitely seen better days—likely splattered with coffee and a few tears for good measure!

Toxic workplaces are like that one ex who just won't quit – they leave you feeling exhausted, questioning your life choices, and wondering if you accidentally stepped on a landmine of bad decisions. But let's be real, you didn't mess up at all! Well, it seems you tripped into a situation that was just not meant for you! Talk about bad luck! And that's precisely what went down with me,

It started, as most terrible ideas do, with an email.

Subject: NEW REQUIREMENT – Weekly Student Engagement Reports

I sighed before I even opened it. The body of the message confirmed my suspicions:

"Dear Educators, in our continued effort to improve student outcomes, all teachers will now be required to submit a "weekly engagement report" detailing each student's level of participation. This will help us track disengaged learners and provide necessary interventions. Your cooperation is appreciated."

I stared at the screen, the weight of the absurdity settled in. I had 140 students across multiple classes. I barely had time to grade their assignments, let alone analyze their weekly enthusiasm levels like some kind of academic sports commentator.

How, exactly, was I supposed to quantify engagement? Was I meant to rank their commitment on a scale from "eager hand - raiser" to "stares into the abyss"? Should I assign a point system? Five points for asking a thoughtful question, two points for nodding at the right moment, and a negative ten for audibly sighing when I announce group work.

At my next staff meeting, the administrator in charge of this new initiative addressed our unspoken resistance.

"This is just about accountability," they assured us. "We need to know who's engaged and who's falling through the cracks."

I raised a hand. "So, to clarify, you want a written, individualized assessment of engagement levels for every student every week?"

A nod.

I pressed on. "And will we be provided with additional time to complete this? Maybe a student - free planning period or reduced admin work to compensate for the added load?"

The administrator chuckled as if I'd suggested recess for teachers. "We know you all manage your time well. This should only take a few extra minutes per class."

I exchanged glances with my colleagues. A few extra minutes? That was six reports per student per month. 840 reports per semester. And I was just one teacher. Multiply that across the whole staff, and they'd have enough data on 'student engagement' to rival the NSA.

I tried a different approach. "What exactly happens if a student is marked as 'disengaged'?"

The administrator hesitated. "Well, we'll discuss potential interventions."

I raised an eyebrow. "So, we're doing all this extra paperwork without a clear action plan for what to do with the data?"

More hesitation. "Well... the data itself is valuable."

I leaned back, crossing my arms. "For who?"

Silence.

By Friday, I had a system. Instead of agonizing over detailed reports, I typed up a generic comment bank:

"Student is actively engaged and participates regularly."

"Student is quietly engaged but does not often volunteer responses."

"Student appears disengaged at times but completes work."

"Student struggles with focus and participation."

Then I *randomly* assigned them.

Because if they were going to waste her time, I was going to waste theirs right back.

There's another case of Lisa who ditched her toxic job and didn't just make it – she absolutely flourished!

Lisa's story is a classic case of flipping the script on a bad experience and turning it into something great! When she strutted out of her toxic job, she didn't just ditch the drama and the stress; she also left behind a piece of herself that she thought had been abducted by aliens and sent to a galaxy far, far away. But with time, patience, and a dash of laughter, Lisa transformed her worst job into the best twist of fate she could have imagined.

"I used to think that my toxic job was the worst thing that ever happened to me," Lisa chuckled, shaking her head in disbelief. "But now I see it was just a little hop on the way to something way cooler. I picked up some nifty tricks for dodging tricky situations, chatting like a pro, and being the ultimate teammate for my coworkers. And let's face it, I also mastered the art of brewing a killer cup of coffee in the break room! Honestly, why bother with a 401k when you can become a master barista instead?"

Lisa's narrative is just one of the countless gems we'll be tossing around in this chapter. We'll hear from employees who've tackled the unthinkable, who've whipped up some clever tricks to handle those MFs, and who've emerged tougher than a two - dollar steak on the other side. We'll share accounts of folks who've transformed their nightmare jobs into laugh - out - loud excursions, who've discovered the secret to tickling their coworkers' funny bones, and who've even turned their bosses into the punchlines of their own jokes.

Consider what happens to Dave, who toiled away in a toxic office where the characters were infamous for their micromanaging antics. But instead of wallowing in despair, Dave thought, "Why not stir the pot a little?" He kicked off a "Micromanaging of the Day" award, where he'd hand out a totally bogus trophy to the champ who could micromanage the hardest that day. It was a tiny act of defiance, but it delivered a much - needed chuckle to the workplace.

Or let's talk about Shelly, who toiled away in a workplace so toxic that the folks there practically had a PhD in scheduling pointless meetings! But rather than endure endless droning, Shelly thought, "Why not spice things up and take charge?" She kicked off a "Meeting Bingo" game, whipping up bingo cards filled with all the classic meeting buzzwords (you know, like "synergy" and "disrupt the status quo"). Every time someone blurted out one of those phrases, Sarah would gleefully cross it off her card like she was on a scavenger hunt for hilarity. It was a tiny rebellion, but it turned those meetings from a snooze - fest into a slightly less torturous experience.

These stories, along with a bunch of others, will prove that even in the grimmest of offices, there's always a twinkle of hope lurking around, probably trying to avoid the coffee machine. You don't have to let your toxic job drag you down; you can rise up, thrive, and maybe even turn it into a stand - up routine! So, if you're feeling like a deflated balloon, totally out of gas, or just ready to nap like a cat in a sunbeam, take a deep breath and remember that you're in good company. There are folks out there who've faced the same shenanigans, and somehow, they've managed to come out on top, probably with a trophy for surviving the chaos. With an injection of wit, a hefty dose of warmth, and a few facts that'll make you feel all the feels, you can totally do it as well!

Rebuilding Confidence: Because You're More Than Just a MF's Plaything

So, you've finally broken free from the grip of your soul - sucking MF and are all set to start piecing together your confidence like a jigsaw puzzle with a few missing pieces! Well, look at you! You've managed to escape unscathed! To the exciting part, which is finding your greatness again and being the rock star you were always intended to be.

Step 1: Take a Break from the MF's Toxicity

Before you look into the rebuilding process, make sure to take a little breather from all that negativity floating around! Imagine it as a tech cleanse, but instead of swiping left on your phone, you're swiping away the relentless nitpicking and condescending remarks. Why not take a little time—be it days, weeks, or even months—to indulge in some self - love and chase after what tickles your fancy?

Step 2: Identify Your Strengths (and Weaknesses)

It's time to have a little heart - to - heart with yourself, buddy! What are your superpowers? What are your not - so - great superpowers? Be real, but cut yourself some slack! Hey, just a friendly reminder: you're not some toy for anyone to mess around with! You're a one - of - a - kind superstar with skills and talents that are totally unmatched. Shine on!

Step 3: Practice Self - Care (and Self - Love)

Self - care isn't only about slapping on face masks and soaking in bubble baths (though, come on, those are pretty fantastic). It's all about juggling your body, feelings, and brain like a circus performer on a unicycle! So, why not pamper yourself with a massage, hit up a yoga class, or dive headfirst into a Netflix marathon? Go on, you deserve it! You totally earned that one!

Step 4: Find Your Tribe

Hang out with folks who boost your spirits and cheer you on! These are the folks who will help you patch up your confidence and give you a friendly nudge about just how awesome you really are! And if you can't track them down in the wild, why not hop into an online community or snag a spot in a support group? It's like a treasure hunt, but with fewer maps and more memes! You're definitely not alone in this wild ride—there's a whole crowd of folks sharing the same rollercoaster of experiences as you!

Step 5: Take Risks and Try New Things

It is time to shake things up and emerge from the comfort of your small bubble. Go on, give something new a whirl! Whether it's a quirky hobby, a wild job, or an outrageous adventure, just jump in and see what kind of chaos unfolds! Hey, just think about it: the absolute worst that could happen is a spectacular flop, but on the flip side, you might just hit the jackpot and uncover a brand-new obsession!

And now, let's hear from someone who's been around the block, collected the souvenirs, and is ready to spill the beans! Meet Bianca, a woman who's danced with chaos and somehow waltzed her way to victory.

I plopped myself next to Bianca, a gal who seemed like she had just wandered off the set of a 90s grunge music video, rocking a flannel shirt and a haircut that practically shouted, "I'm a rebel, Dottie!" But underneath her tough shell, Bianca had a story to share - one of survival, durability, and piecing together her confidence after facing the ultimate jerk.

Bianca's eyes flashed like disco balls as she recounted her experience, her voice oozing with playful irony and wit. "I used to think that my MF was the absolute worst thing that ever happened to me," she said, giving a dramatic eye roll. "But now I see it was just a little hiccup on my grand adventure." I mean, who needs a job that drains the life out of you when you can have a life - draining MF instead, am I right?

But let's be real, Bianca's experience was a real doozy! She had to deal with a never - ending circus of belittling, micromanaging, and an overall vibe that felt like working for someone who thrived on turning her daily grind into a comedy of errors. But after escaping her toxic job, Bianca discovered that her confidence had taken a little vacation and forgot to leave a forwarding address. She felt like a ship without a compass, drifting through a storm of her own insecurities, hoping to bump into something that made sense.

That's when she hilariously tripped over the idea of volunteering. Bianca jumped into the world of a local animal shelter, and out of nowhere, she discovered she was doing something that made her feel like a superhero in a fur‑covered cape. She was out there lending a hand, changing the world, and ‑ let's be real ‑ she was doing it all without someone breathing down her neck like an overzealous life coach.

"I know it sounds a bit off, but volunteering totally gave my confidence a makeover," Bianca said with a casual shrug. "You know, when you lend a hand to others, it hits you that you're not just some tiny gear in a giant robot. You're a fabulous individual bursting with skills, talents, and a mission that even superheroes would envy. And that's a feeling that packs quite the punch.

Resources for Ongoing Development: Because You're Not Stuck in Neutral (Even If It Feels Like It)

Congratulations! You've dodged the drama and are now ready to escape the chaos! You've escaped the clutches of doom! But now, you're in a bit of a pickle: how to keep cruising ahead, even when it feels like you're just spinning your wheels in neutral.

We must admit it, leaving a toxic job can be a major setback. It's like pressing the big red reset button on your career, and poof! You're right back at the starting line, wondering where all the snacks went! But guess what? You're in good company. And well, you're not glued to the spot like a lost sock in the dryer. There's a treasure trove of resources just waiting for you to get your feet in and keep that brain of yours growing and grooving.

The Best Revenge is Living Well (and Succeeding Despite the Odds)

Remember, the best way to get back at your MF is to succeed despite them. And the best way to do that is to keep learning and growing. So, here are a few resources to get you started:

- Online courses: Websites like Coursera, Udemy, and LinkedIn Learning offer a wide range of courses on everything from coding to marketing to leadership.

- Professional associations: Joining a professional association can be a great way to network, learn from others, and stay up - to - date on the latest industry trends.

- Books and podcasts: There are plenty of great books and podcasts out there on topics like productivity, leadership, and career development.

- Mentorship: Find someone who's been in your shoes and can offer guidance and support.

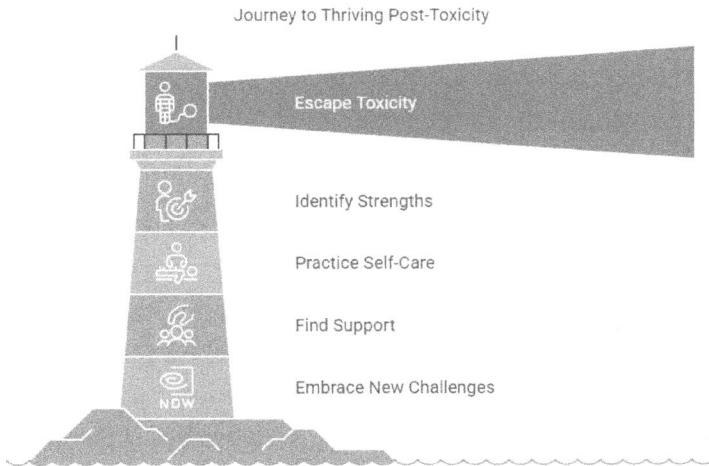

Journey to Thriving Post-Toxicity

Escape Toxicity

Identify Strengths

Practice Self-Care

Find Support

Embrace New Challenges

But What If I'm Stuck?

We've all had those moments - feeling like we're in quicksand, not sure if we should wiggle our toes or just give up and start a new career as a professional couch potato. But here's the kicker: you're not glued to the spot!

You're on a little break, aren't you? And the most hilarious way to get unstuck is to do something, anything really!

Alright, take a deep breath, crank up that motivational playlist that makes you feel like a superhero, and start waddling your way towards those goals, one tiny step at a time! Whether you're descending into an online course, schmoozing at a networking event, or giving your resume a little makeover, just get moving! And don't forget, the ultimate payback is thriving like a champ - and crushing it even when the universe throws you curveballs.

And now, let's hear from someone who's been around the block, collected the souvenirs, and is rocking the t - shirt like a champ. Meet Tim, a fellow who decided to grab his career by the horns after escaping the clutches of his toxic job.

Tim's journey is a wild ride of bouncing back and sheer willpower! After escaping his toxic job, he felt like a ship adrift at sea, wondering if he should start a new career or just take up competitive napping instead. But instead of throwing in the towel, he thought, "Why not stir the pot a little?" He jumped into online courses, mingled at networking shindigs, and gave his resume a makeover. And before he knew it, he snagged a job that actually appreciated his genius ideas!

"I was stuck in a rut, feeling like I was on a treadmill with no power," Tim said, shaking his head. "But then it hit me like a pie in the face that I actually had the power to change my own destiny. I jumped into online courses, and out of nowhere, I found myself with a shiny new sense of purpose. Who knew learning could be so enlightening? I was learning, growing, and cha - cha - ing my way forward - and let me tell you, it felt like a party."

Chapter 08:
Case Studies: Lessons from the Trenches

If your workplace resembles a scene from a low - budget horror flick, with bright lights that flash alarmingly and printers hovering like they're auditioning for a concerto of whines about the latest "genius" plans from the big boss, then my friend, you absolutely need to get into this chapter and definitely don't even think about skipping it! Now the tension is thicker than a plot twist, and the coffee? Oh, it's perpetually tepid! Here, employees integrate through a maze of nonsense, sidestepping the antics of their MFs like pros in a wild round of corporate dodgeball.

We are further going to dissect the zany universe of workplace shenanigans, sharing the true tales that uncover the comedy and chaos of handling those characters. These stories aren't just a hoot; they're loaded with nuggets of wisdom that can help you dodge the blunders and come out with your wits—and perhaps a chuckle or two—still intact.

In - Depth Case Studies

Let's cut to the chase: working under an MF is like being on a game show where the rules flip - flop every five minutes, and the grand prize is just making it through the day without losing your mind. But hey, no need to panic! We're here to spill the beans on those brave souls who took on the MF music and somehow made it out with their sanity intact! These case studies are not merely cautionary tales; they're lessons wrapped in giggles, garnished with a sprinkle of "Did that really just happen?"

Case Study 1: The Email Tyrant

Meet Karen, a marketing manager who found herself in the hilarious predicament of working for someone who thought emails were the holy grail of communication. Oh, you know the kind: the one who fires off a 10 - paragraph email at 11 PM, loaded with passive - aggressive gems and a subject line that scream, "Urgent: Your Immediate Attention Required."

Karen remembers the day she got an email with the delightful subject line "Your Incompetence is Showing." "I seriously thought someone was pulling my leg," she said, shaking her head in disbelief. "But no, it was just another day in the life of my magnificent fiasco. I mean, who needs a motivational poster when you have someone who can turn your day upside down with just one email?"

What's the takeaway from all this? Don't let someone's email rants rain on your parade. Instead, take a deep breath, hit "reply all" with a clever quip (but maybe keep it in your drafts), and remember that their need for control is just a peek into their own insecurities.

Case Study 2: The Micromanaging Maestro

Next up is Dave, a software developer who found himself in the clutches of an MF who turned micromanagement into an extreme sport. "My MF would totally hover over my shoulder while I coded," Dave said, giving an exaggerated eye roll. "I felt like I was trapped in a particularly cringe - worthy episode of 'Big Brother' where the grand prize was just my dwindling sanity."

One day, Dave thought it would be a brilliant idea to see just how far he could push the boundaries of his MF's micromanagement skills. He began hammering away at his keyboard, unleashing a thrilling storm of nonsense into his code, just to see how long it would take for the poor soul to catch on. "I was halfway through a line of code that read 'banana hammock' when my brain finally hit the eject button," he chuckled. "Well, I suppose I should've realized that 'banana hammock' wasn't exactly going to be a hit in a professional setting."

The moral of the story? If you ever find yourself in the clutches of a micromanaging overlord, just remember, you hold the ultimate trump card: your independence! Time to break free and show them who's boss! Whether it's through a good laugh, a cheeky shrug, or just nailing your tasks while they throw a fit, you can totally outlast the chaos.

Case Study 3: The Meeting Overlord

Now let's get into the history of Cyndi, who toiled away for a company that had a bizarre love affair with meetings—seriously, they were practically dating them! "I swear, my MF thought meetings were the magic cure for every issue," she said, rolling her eyes. "We had meetings to strategize on how to schedule more meetings about meetings." It was like being stuck on a rollercoaster that just wouldn't stop, and the only thing waiting at the end was a giant pie in the face!

On a particularly memorable Tuesday, Cyndi thought it was high time to make her voice heard. She whipped up a PowerPoint presentation called "The Meeting That Could Have Been an Email." "I presented it during our weekly meeting, and oh boy, the expressions on their faces were absolutely hilarious," she laughed. "I even whipped up a pie chart illustrating just how much time we've spent in meetings compared to doing actual work. Spoiler alert: the pie is mostly empty!"

Also, don't forget the *professional development days*—an event more pointless than a PowerPoint with 58 slides and no "skip" button. You ever sat through a four - hour workshop meeting where an MF Reads. Every. Single. Word. Off a PowerPoint - like they're performing Shakespeare?

Once, I sat through an entire "Student Engagement Strategies" meeting presented by someone who had never taught a day in their life but had watched at least two TED Talks on the subject. They spent an hour explaining that "students enjoy being engaged" like they'd just cracked the Da Vinci Code.

And let's not forget the mandatory icebreakers.

"We're going to start today by going around and saying one interesting fact about ourselves!"

"Ma'am, we are thirty minutes into our lunch break, underpaid, exhausted, and running on spite and caffeine. The most interesting fact I can give you right now is that I am one awkward team - building activity away from faking a medical emergency."

And if you dare to point out that these sessions are a massive waste of time? Oh no. That's negativity. That's "a lack of collaborative spirit."

Case Study 4: Data, Data, Data!

Speaking from my personal experience, if numbers had a fan club, MMF would be the president, vice president, and treasurer. They're obsessed with tracking every possible metric—test scores, attendance rates, bathroom passes, the number of times a kid blinks in class. But do they actually *understand* the data? Absolutely not.

"According to our numbers, student performance dips after lunch. What can we do to fix this?"

"Well, maybe because they just ate a giant tray of carbs and are in a food coma?"

"Hmm. Let's add another assessment right after lunch to measure engagement."

This is the same person who suggests that more standardized testing will "help us better understand student needs" and thinks that a graph will solve all educational problems. They don't actually understand it, but they love using it to make teachers miserable.

One year, my MF decided that "bathroom pass usage" was an indicator of classroom management skills.

Yes, bathroom pass usage.

Forget lesson effectiveness. Forget real learning outcomes. Nope. If more than 8% of my students had to pee on any given day, I was clearly a failure as an educator.

I wanted to submit my own Management Data Report™ in return:

- Percentage of useful feedback given: 0%

- Percentage of times emails were ignored: 87%

- Percentage of their "strategies" that actually worked: - 14%

And let's not forget the testing season.

Every year, we were expected to increase student test scores despite the fact that:

- The tests change every year.

- The students couldn't care less about these tests.

- The scores are used exclusively to punish teachers rather than help students.

It got to the point where I started taking bets on what random metric my MF would pull out of thin air next. "Amount of oxygen consumed per student" as an indicator of classroom engagement? "The number of times a kid blinks during a lesson" to gauge interest levels?

It was only a matter of time.

What is the lesson to be learned from this? If you ever feel like you're sinking in a tidal wave of utterly useless meetings, don't hesitate to raise your hand and shout for help! Sprinkle a little wit to get your message across, and who knows what might happen? You could be the spark that ignites a full - blown uprising against those wild meeting shenanigans!

Key Takeaways

So, you've had your fill of run - ins with those characters, and now you're scratching your head about what to do (or what to avoid) if you stumble into a similar mess again. Don't sweat it! We're here to squeeze the juice from our case studies into tasty little morsels of advice that you can actually use—because honestly, who wants to be the headliner in the next "What Not to Do at Work" documentary?

1. Document Everything

If there's one nugget of wisdom to snag from Tom's wild ride with the Praise Thief, it's this: jot it down! Imagine it as your own little book of office antics and hilarious escapades. Every email, every meeting note, and every time your MF tries to pull a fast one and claim your genius as their own—write it all down! You'll need a paper trail that could rival a CVS receipt when it's time to back up your brilliance!

2. Trust Your Gut

Enter Lisa, who discovered that ignoring red flags is just like pretending a fire alarm is playing your favorite tune—sooner or later, you're going to feel the heat! "I really believed I could turn my MF around," she said, giving a dramatic shake of her head. "Well, plot twist: I totally failed." If your gut is throwing a fit and waving red flags, you might want to pay attention! Your gut is like that buddy who can sniff out a sketchy situation from a mile away. Don't sell yourself short; you're not some last - minute bargain bin find!

3. Build Your Support Squad

Remember Tom's little alliance? That's the kind of buddy - buddy vibe you want to whip up! Keep your circle filled with coworkers who've got your back and aren't shy about pointing out the ridiculousness! It's like assembling the Avengers, but instead of flying and fighting villains, you're armed with spreadsheets and an endless supply of coffee mugs. Join forces to take on the ridiculousness of the office, and who knows, you might just kick off a support group named "MF Survivors Anonymous."

4. Set Boundaries

If your MF is trying to crash your personal space party—emotionally or physically—throw up those boundaries like a champ! "Oh, absolutely not! I refuse to be the hero who saves the day on a Friday just because you thought it would be a brilliant idea to have a 'brainstorming session' that could have easily been an email," you might say. Hey, just a friendly reminder: your time is precious, and you're definitely not a human welcome mat for anyone's random requests!

5. Know When to Walk Away

Sometimes, the smartest move is to grab your bags and make a beeline for the door! If your MF is turning your work life into a circus, it might be time to unleash your inner Houdini! "I realized I was more stressed than a cat at a dance party," Lisa recounted. "Well, I finally jumped off the diving board!" Figuring out when to make a grand exit is just as crucial as deciding when to throw on your boxing gloves and duke it out!

Keep in mind, dealing with a toxic workplace is no stroll through the tulips, but with the right game plan, you can come out with your sanity—and perhaps a chuckle or two—still in one piece.

Interviews with Experts and Survivors

Come to the wisdom corner, where we've assembled a quirky bunch of experts and survivors who've tangoed with MFs and survived to share their hilarious stories. These fearless warriors have transformed their workplace nightmares into golden lessons, all while maintaining their hilarious outlook on life. So better grab your popcorn, because this is about to get hilariously crazy!

Expert Insights: The Pros Weigh In

Dr. S. "The Workplace Whisperer" Thompson

Dr. Thompson, the workplace whisperer, has witnessed every office shenanigan imaginable. "Dealing with MFs is like trying to teach a cat to fetch," she joked. "Oh, come on! It's like trying to teach a cat to fetch – it's just not in the cards, and you'll only end up pulling your hair out!" What pearls of wisdom does she have to share? "Concentrate on the one thing you can actually manage—how you respond." If your MF is having a meltdown, just don't get sucked in! Instead, tap into your inner zen master and let it slide off your back like a duck in a water park!

Mark "The Career Coach" Johnson

Mark has dedicated years to guiding folks through the wild jungle of toxic workplaces. "Imagine your MF as a haircut gone horribly wrong," he said, laughing heartily. "It may seem like a disaster right now, but hang tight, it's just a phase!" "You can always outgrow it!" His number one piece of advice? "Network as if your career is hanging by a thread—because it totally is!" Make friends beyond your MF's little bubble! "You never know when you might find yourself in a pickle!"

Survivor Stories: From Chaos to Clarity

Jessica "The Resilient" Martinez

Jessica worked under an MF who thrived on chaos. "Every day felt like I was in a reality show called 'Survivor: Office Edition,'" she recalled. "But I learned to adapt. I started keeping a 'win' journal, where I'd jot down my daily victories, no matter how small. It was my way of reminding myself that I was still capable of greatness, even if my MF was trying to dim my light."

David "The Escape Artist" Chen

David's story is a real knee - slapper! "I was trapped in a job where my boss would snatch my glory and then toss me under the bus during performance reviews," he said. "So, I thought, why not flip the script?" I began my job hunt while still clocking in at my current gig! It felt like I was in a spy movie, but instead of chasing down villains, I was just on a mission to keep my sanity intact! What pearls of wisdom does he have to share? "Always have a plan to make a swift getaway." "You just never know when it'll come in handy!"

Lisa "The Phoenix" Reynolds

Lisa's experience was like a wild ride at an amusement park, full of ups, downs, and unexpected twists! "I felt like I was dating a cactus, all prickly and no cuddles," she admitted. "But instead of sulking, I decided to enroll in a course on conflict resolution." It was like trying to decipher a secret code while juggling flaming torches! Out of nowhere, I found myself gracefully tiptoeing through the chaotic circus of MF shenanigans. What did she learn from all this? "Put your money where your mouth is—into your own brain!" Knowledge is like a superhero cape; it can help you soar above the chaos and confusion!

Well, look at that! An amusing selection of tales and wisdom from those who've tackled the MF music and lived to tell the history! If you're in the mood for some solid tips or just want to chuckle, these interviews dish out a nice mix of both! Hey, just a friendly reminder that you're not the only brave soul conquering this crazy office jungle!

How to effectively manage a challenging workplace dynamic?

Email Tyrant

Improve communication efficiency

Micromanaging Maestro

Foster employee independence

⌣◦

Chapter 09:
The Office Olympics

An open - space office bathed in blinding white lighting, the constant rhythm of clicking keyboards in the background, faint phone conversations, and occasional strained laughter at a manager's not - so - hilarious jokes. On the surface, everything seems normal, but beneath the polished facade of professional calm lies a chaotic battlefield where passive - aggressive emails are the weapons of choice, whispered gossip fuels the fire of corporate survival, daily antics of petty power plays and office politics keep everyone on their toes, all while someone desperately tries to remind everyone who's wearing the crown. Welcome to the Office Olympics, where training is as uncommon as spotting a stapler in a paperless office, yet somehow, everyone ends up in the competition whether they like it or not! There are no grand openings, no raucous applause, and definitely no shiny medals—unless you count the one in your mind that says, "I made it through another day of this circus."

The reins of this wild circus are in the hands of a bunch of MFs, playing referee in a game that nobody even wants to enter! Equipped with their inflated egos and a flair for theatrics, they take the stage at events like "The Blame Game," where accountability is a sizzling hot potato that everyone dodges, and "The Favoritism Olympics," where workplace peace takes a backseat to the relentless race of favoritism - fueled rivalries. And who could forget "The Communication Blackout," a masterclass in keeping everyone in the dark while pointing fingers at them for being out of the loop? These games are less about hitting the jackpot and more about watching how many hoops employees can leap through without landing in a pile of frustration and passive - aggressive Slack banter.

The rules for the Office Olympics are as clear as a foggy day, and the MFMs are the undisputed kings of chaos. Strategies are like a day when you can't find your car keys, goals are as unpredictable as a cat on a hot tin roof, and the referees (or should I say those mischievous folks) appear to be the ones playing with a deck that's definitely not in your favor! It's not just about teamwork; it's about dodging disaster and keeping your head in the game! Who needs gold medals when you can hunt for the real treasures? A tiny sliver of sanity, a brief moment of peace, or the sheer joy of outsmarting someone who thought they had it all figured out. Now that's the real prize! How much do I need to fork over to jump into the shenanigans? A never - ending stash of sticky notes that could double as a passive - aggressive art exhibit, all while my patience takes a nosedive!

But don't worry—you're not the only contestant in this corporate circus of survival! This chapter is your ultimate survival manual, brimming with playful "training modules" designed to help you move around the choppy waters of office politics while keeping a grin on your face. We'll plunge into the rules of engagement, untangle the quirky tactics of MFMs, and arm you with some snazzy strategies to sidestep the landmines they generously scatter along your career path.

Satirical Training Modules

Mastering "The Blame Game"

This is your go - to guide to handling "The Blame Game," one of the most infamous Office Olympics events. Picture responsibility as a piping hot potato, and the MFM as the star quarterback, ready to hurl it at anyone who dares to come close! The rules are as clear as their leadership abilities: when things go awry (which, let's face it, happens more often than not), the goal is to ensure the blame gets flung around like a game of hot potato, never settling anywhere close to them.

- **Misdirection Mastery:** An MF will point fingers faster than a magician pulls a rabbit out of a hat. "I asked *you* to confirm the deadline," they'll insist, as if their original email wasn't more of a puzzling enigma than a straightforward instruction.

- **Selective Amnesia:** Ah yes, the timeless tactic—because why bother owning up to anything when you can just hit the forget button, am I right? It's quite a talent they have for conveniently forgetting anything that might land them in a bit of trouble! That's quite the unique skill you've got there! "I don't remember giving that the green light," they'll chime in, as if their memory is on a nightly vacation, leaving behind a deserted brain!"

- **The Blame Cascade:** When one underperformer isn't enough to satisfy their thirst for scapegoats, they'll just drag everyone else into the mess, because why take responsibility alone when you can spread the misery around? Wow, who knew a little typo could turn into a catastrophic circus for the whole department? Bravo!

Key Skills to Win "The Blame Game"

Selective Memory Tactics: The first rule of the blame game is never to get caught flat - footed. Develop the art of feigned forgetfulness and impeccable timing to deflect responsibility. Like, the *"Oh, I Thought You Knew!" Maneuver.* In the middle of all this madness, just casually drop a sweet, "Oh, I thought you had that covered already!" The plan is to sprinkle just the right amount of uncertainty so you can dodge the heat while still pretending you're not totally out of the loop.

Documentation Ninja: This is your ultimate weapon—a paper trail so airtight it could survive a legal audit. The trick? Document *everything*.

- Always *timestamp important communications*. If a deadline changes, an email with "Just confirming the new timeline as discussed today at 10:37 AM" works wonders.

- Use professional - sounding language to *subtly toss blame back* where it belongs. For example, "Per your suggestion during the February 15th meeting, I've prioritized Task A over Task B. Should we realign priorities?"

- Always *copy yourself on emails* and store them in a special folder for quick retrieval. If the MFM tries to pull a "You should have known," you can pull out receipts faster than a magician produces rabbits.

Mastering "The Favoritism Olympics"

This isn't a simple race to the finish line; it's a carefully devised parade of inequity, where some employees are handed golden tickets while others are weighed down with sandbags. The MF is both referee and competitor, ensuring that favoritism keeps everyone else off balance. Here's how it plays out:

- **The Chosen Ones:** Employees who always laugh at every joke, nod enthusiastically at every nonsensical idea, and somehow manage to be the boss's favorite lunch buddies. These "favorites" are showered with plum projects, public praise, and leniency, creating a sharp divide among the team.

- **Pitting Employees Against Each Other:** The MF stirs up competition among team members, either overtly ("Whoever delivers the best pitch gets the spotlight") or covertly (giving one employee inside information that others aren't privy to). This fosters a cutthroat environment that prioritizes backstabbing over collaboration.

Key Skills to Win "The Favoritism Olympics"

- **Strategic Fake Laughing**: Let's be honest; most manager jokes land somewhere between *dad jokes* and *cringe - worthy anecdotes*. But your laugh? It should be a masterpiece. For minor quips, deploy a soft chuckle, and for moments when your MF thinks they've dropped comedy gold, bring out the big guns—a hearty laugh with a perfectly timed fake snort.

- **Subtle Flattery Disguised as Team Spirit**: Direct flattery makes coworkers side - eye you like you just got a promotion for bringing coffee. The workaround? Turn your compliments into team - focused gems. When complimenting your MF, include all your team members, such as, "We're so lucky to have someone with your experience steering the ship!" or "Your presentation helped us all see the bigger picture." These lines build goodwill with your boss while reassuring coworkers you haven't joined Team Suck - Up.

Mastering "The Communication Blackout"

Imagine this: A vital project is underway, but key details—like deadlines, deliverables, or even the ultimate goal—are nowhere to be found. Welcome to the Communication Blackout, where the MF reigns supreme as the keeper of all information and shares it only on a need - to - know basis (and you *just happened to be nowhere near that need - to - know list*). The chaos usually unfolds like this:

- **The Information Bottleneck:** Instead of sharing updates with the team, the MF hoards them, creating a culture of confusion. Deadlines are missed, priorities are misaligned, and when the inevitable chaos ensues, guess who gets blamed? Not them.

- **Vague Instructions:** When MFs do communicate, it's often in the form of cryptic, incomplete directives. "Make sure the presentation pops," they'll say, leaving you to wonder if they mean bold graphics, a killer conclusion, or literally embedding confetti cannons in the slide deck.

- **The Blame Shift:** After the blackout creates inevitable problems, the MF swoops right back in. "Why didn't you confirm this earlier?" they'll ask, conveniently omitting that no one even knew it was their responsibility.

Key Skills to Win "The Blame Game"

- **The Power of Over - Communication:** MFs often issue vague or incomplete instructions to maintain control. Counter this by always confirming details in writing. Examples: "Just to make sure we're aligned; do you mean **submitting the report by Friday** or **providing a draft for review by Friday?**" or "I want to confirm that this report is due by Thursday at 3 PM. Let me know if that's incorrect." This tactic serves two purposes: it forces the MF to clarify their expectations and gives you written evidence if they try to shift blame later.

- **Reverse Withholding:** Beat MFs at their own game by sharing critical information with the team before they can weaponize it. For instance, if you learn about a deadline change, email the team: "Heads up: I just heard the deadline for the marketing campaign has moved to next Friday. Let's regroup to make sure we're on track!"

Disclaimers: Proceed with Caution

Mastering Office Survival Skills

05	Achieve Resilience
04	Navigate Office Politics
03	Maintain Well-being
02	Reverse Withholding
01	Over-Communication

While these strategies are meant to help you wade through the wild waters of the Office Olympics, they're not about transforming you into a corporate gladiator battling for your life in the cubicle coliseum. This is all about staying alive, not being the boss of the jungle. The goal here is to simplify your work life, not to kick off a Shakespearean soap opera filled with backstabbing and plot twists. Channel your inner diplomat, not your inner schemer plotting moves in the castle of chaos. Also, keep in mind petty victories can backfire. Absolutely, a perfectly timed joke or a sly little rebellion can definitely deliver a delightful dose of joy. Just keep in mind, a career that actually means something is like a fine wine – it takes time to mature, not a quick shot of something that might leave you with a hangover of regret.

Make your mental health the VIP of your life. Treat it like a celebrity that needs all the attention and care it can get! Toxic environments can really suck the life out of you! Even though these strategies might lighten the load, there's no trick in the book that can substitute for the value of your well - being. If your job feels like a never - ending energy vampire or a personal morale black hole, it might be time to take a good look at your situation and whip up a grand escape plan.

In the end, just remember to keep it real and don't bite off more than you can chew! Write it down, but don't turn it into a battle tool. Keeping a paper trail is super important, but if you wave it around like a sword, you might just start a paperwork war. The aim is to keep yourself safe, not to kick off a dramatic office duel. Just remember, there's a delicate balance between defending yourself and going a bit overboard like a kid on a sugar rush! Toxic managers are like puppeteers, pulling strings and turning even the tiniest hint of defiance into a full - blown drama. They may forget their own blunders faster than a goldfish, but when it comes to your tiny missteps, they remember them with the accuracy of a courtroom transcript.

Closing Ceremony

The Office Olympics, a wacky, tiring, and sometimes side - splitting event, can seem like a wild marathon of ridiculousness. You're balancing absurd expectations, sidestepping blame like a pro, and tiptoeing through the maze of office politics—all while keeping up the act of being a total professional. But here's the bright side: if you can endure the wild shenanigans of those characters, you'll emerge with a skillset that rivals that of a hostage negotiator, a crisis manager, and a top - notch diplomat all mashed together!

You'll have mastered the art of wading through murky waters like a graceful hippo, transforming a toxic environment into your personal chessboard, all while keeping your sanity intact as everyone else is losing theirs like socks in a dryer. You'll figure out when to chime in, when to zip it, and how to twist any scenario to your favor without losing your moral compass. It's like a game of social chess, but with fewer pawns and more snacks.

So, off you go, brave reader, and snag that survival medal—it may not be shiny gold, but hey, it's still a trophy for making it through the chaos. You've dodged the clowns, navigated the fog, and outsmarted the illusions, and now you're all set for whatever wild ride comes next. Whether you decide to hang out or plot your grand escape, you'll walk away with priceless wisdom and a skin so tough, it could probably withstand a bear hug from a rhinoceros.

Chapter 10:
The Art of Passive - Aggressive Resistance

The art of passive - aggressive resistance—a clumsy shuffle that needs the finesse of a toddler on roller skates and the slyness of a raccoon rummaging through trash. It's like attempting to dance on a tightrope while juggling flaming swords and wearing a clown wig. So, when you're stuck with a manager who thinks chaos is a management style and micromanagement is their love language, resisting the urge to push back is like trying to ignore a chocolate cake at a weight loss seminar—good luck with that! Defiance, on the other hand, is like waving a red flag in front of a bull. You're just asking for trouble, and trust me, nobody wants to be the next big joke around here.

So, how do you tiptoe into the realm of passive - aggressive resistance without having your head served on a platter? Welcome to the world of half - hearted defiance, where you can whisper your opinions without actually having the guts to shout them out—or at least not in a way that would get you kicked out of the room. Imagine a battlefield at work, where your only ammo is your sharp tongue, a heavy dose of sarcasm, and the perfect eye roll that says, "Really?"

MFs are like those inflatable lawn decorations that show up every holiday season, all flashy and full of hot air, but deflate the moment you poke them. They're like a marching band in a library—loud, obnoxious, and somehow always managing to spread out like they own the place. But just like those decorations, they're also a total disaster waiting to happen. A little jab here, a soft shove there, and boom—they're all deflated while you strut around like you just won the lottery of life.

Surviving the MFs Maze

MF don't answer emails. They don't show up when a fight breaks out. They don't respond when you need backup. I am sure teachers can totally relate to this. Our classroom would have been a *Hunger Games* arena all year, and they would be nowhere to be found. But the second, it's time for evaluations? They materialize out of thin air.

You've been running a flawless, engaging lesson all week—students debating, collaborating, actually *learning*. But when does the administrator decide to pop in?

The exact moment when:

- Half the class is staring blankly at the ceiling like they're contemplating the meaning of life.

- Someone in the back is engaged... in trying to turn a paperclip into a makeshift shiv.

- And, of course, the one time you *do* call on a student, they respond with a deep sigh and, *"Wait... what are we doing?"*

The management scribbles something on their clipboard and slides you a neatly worded dagger:

"Students appeared disengaged. Consider making lessons more interactive."

You consider making the note *disappear* into the nearest shredder—or possibly setting it on fire.

But remember: THEY need YOU. Schools don't function without teachers. MFAs might pretend they're in charge, but without you, their kingdom collapses.

And when all else fails?

Just remember—WiFi 'outages' are a teacher's best friend.

It works every time.

Alright, before we wade into the swamp of passive - aggressive nonsense, let's get straight on what we're actually talking about. These folks are the kind who flourish in chaos, brandishing their influence like a toddler with a crayon—sloppy and completely oblivious to the aftermath. They're the kind of people who micromanage like it's an Olympic sport, flipping priorities around like a DJ trying to impress a crowd, and they belittle your hard work as if they're practicing for a part in the cringiest sitcom ever. So, how do you stand up to their nonsense without landing yourself in a world of trouble?

Let's start by discussing the importance of the status update. Imagine this: your genius boss, in all their infinite wisdom, has just declared that the project you've poured your heart and soul into for weeks is now a "low priority." Why? Because they've had a lightbulb moment about "synergizing the core competencies of our value proposition." Classic move, right? (As if that makes any sense, huh?) Instead of flailing around like a fish out of water or, heaven forbid, turning it into a full - on scream fest, how about you whip up a status update that actually gets your point across without playing the blame game?

Let's talk about Jason for a second. Jason was the undisputed champion of backhanded compliments and subtle sabotage. When his boss kept changing priorities like a toddler who just discovered a new toy, Jason whipped up status updates that were as stealthy as a ninja trying to blend in at a library. His updates sound like a GPS that can't decide where to go—

always recalculating and never getting anywhere fast. Oh, look at you, waiting for priorities to be clarified like it's some kind of cosmic revelation.

Wow, look at you trying to make an entrance! Boom? More like a whimper. The message was crystal clear: Jason wasn't the problem here; it was those clowns who were busy playing hopscotch with the project timeline. It's like mailing a postcard from the kingdom of "I'm perfect, it's definitely you." without even bothering to voice it. Bravo! Oh, and let me guess, there's a "best part"? That's rich! It's all dressed up in a shiny, polite bow that even your boss, who probably thinks they're the king of the world, can't dispute.

Oh sure, because nothing says "I'm important" like hitting send on an email at just the right moment. You know the type—the kind that looks so harmless, it could easily pass for a cheerful postcard from the neighbor you never wanted to talk to. But beneath that so - called friendly facade is a message sharp enough to slice through tension like a butter knife through, well, butter.

What if your boss, the master of chaos, just dropped an email with a new set of "guidelines" that are so convoluted they make a cat trying to solve a Rubik's Cube look like a genius? How about you try a "Did you just fall off the stupid tree and hit every branch on the way down?" Oh, come on, we all know that's the first thing you thought of! You could at least try to sound a little more original and say, "Thanks for clearing that up!" Just to make sure we're all in the loop, can you confirm if we're sticking to the original timeline or if we've chosen to accept the disruption and go with the 'let's wing it' strategy?"

This way, you're not just making your point but also giving your boss a chance to untangle their own jumbled mess of ideas. Good luck with that! It's like giving them a mirror and saying, "Hey, take a good look!" without even breaking a sweat.

Oh, and how could we overlook the classic excuse of "I'm just following orders"? Truly a masterpiece of accountability, isn't it? When your boss turns into a control freak and hovers over you like a hawk, it's hard not to want to throw a tantrum. But instead, maybe try not to be so obvious for once. When they start breathing down your neck about every little detail, just hit them with, "I appreciate your input!" like it's the most groundbreaking thing they've ever said. Seriously, it's like they think they're the CEO of your life or something. "Oh, how noble of you! Following guidance like it's a treasure map, huh? Good luck with that!"

"Look at you, trying to stroke their ego while also dropping the hint that you're not psychic. Bravo, really. What a masterclass in diplomacy!" It's like saying, "I'm totally my own person, but I'll prance around like a marionette as long as you keep the beats coming."

Oh sure, passive - aggressive resistance isn't just about being a wordsmith; it's also about those tiny annoyances that can send someone straight to the edge of sanity. Oh, look at you, trying to sound all profound with your fancy term "delayed response." What's next, a TED Talk on how to take your time to think? Bravo, really. You must be the life of the party with that one. When your boss hits you up with an urgent email like they're the king of the world, just sit back and take your sweet time responding. They'll love that! Oh, look at you, either swamped with tasks or just living your best life with that fancy cup of coffee. Must be nice! Well, look at you, playing the waiting game like a pro. Just let them simmer in their own impatience; it's not like they have anything better to do, right?

And when you finally decide to grace us with a response, please make sure it's accompanied by a smiley face emoji, because we all know how much that adds to your charm. Nothing screams "I'm totally chill, but you're a hot mess" quite like slapping an emoji in the mix. It's like trying to dress up a sundae that's already a puddle because your anxiety is throwing a heatwave.

Alright, let's take a quick detour to talk about Jason for a second. After his genius - level status updates, he thought he could actually elevate his game. Spoiler alert: he couldn't. He thinks he's a comedian now, tossing around lines like, "As we navigate this ever - changing landscape, I'll be sure to keep my compass handy!" Newsflash: nobody's laughing, buddy. Oh, how charming! It's like saying, "Congrats, you're the chaos creator here, not me," but with a sprinkle of sugar on top to keep it all friendly. Classic move!

In the realm of backhanded compliments and subtle jabs, humor is the only ally you've got left. It's like a flimsy shield that barely keeps out the arrows of negativity, but hey, at least it lets you laugh at how ridiculous everything is. Good luck with that! When you can chuckle at the mess, it really strips away some of its drama, doesn't it? Oh sure, because who wouldn't want to dive headfirst into a circus of nonsense? Feel it like it's your long - lost relative at a family reunion—awkward, but you can't escape it! When your boss decides to pull another ridiculous stunt, just grin and remind yourself, "This is going to be the highlight of my next happy hour rant."

Oh, look at you, trying to be all clever with your "strategic compliment." What's next, a masterclass in flattery? When your boss is throwing a tantrum, it's hard not to just roll your eyes and whisper some sweet nothings about their attitude. Wow, it's impressive how you manage to keep so many balls in the air without dropping any... yet! Keep it up, and you might just become a circus act. It's like watching a circus performer, but somehow even more clumsy and disorganized. Bravo! This not only points out their wild approach but also hilariously underscores just how absurd the whole thing is. Oh sure, a win - win—like saying a two - headed coin is a good investment. Good luck with that!

And if all else fails, you can always fall back on the timeless excuse of "I'm just here for the paycheck." Real original, buddy. When those clowns start to get on your nerves, just remember you're not here to be a superhero; you're just here to cash in a paycheck and maybe score some free snacks while you're at it. This mindset is like a breath of fresh air—if that air was filled with the scent of your last bad decision. It lets you take a breather and see the madness as just another Tuesday in the life of an office gladiator. I'd say do well done!

In the end, passive - aggressive resistance is just a fancy way of saying you want to be stubborn while pretending you're not losing your mind. Good luck with that balancing act! It's all about cracking jokes and flexing those creative muscles to wade through the swamp of office drama without getting pulled into the quicksand. So, the next time you encounter some clown hell - bent on turning your life into a circus, just remember: you've got the power to push back, and you can do it while flashing a grin and a snappy comeback that'll leave them speechless.

As we dive into this chapter, get ready to uncover even more sneaky tactics and strategies for perfecting the fine art of passive - aggressive resistance. Because who doesn't love a good backhanded approach? Oh sure, because nothing screams "subtle rebellion" like diving into the vast world of MFs. What a wild ride that must be! Get ready, because this rollercoaster is about to take you for a spin you won't forget—if you can handle it!

Oh, look at you, the maestro of backhanded compliments and subtle defiance! Bravo! If you really believed we were finished with our sneaky little tricks, you clearly don't know us at all. Oh, please, you call that warming up? I've seen better starts from a microwave! In this section, we'll dive into some clever moves to help you handle the ridiculous demands of your Middle - Finger Managers (MFs) while trying to keep your sanity from completely flying out the window. Alright, Picasso, let's see what kind of masterpiece of mischief you can whip up with your little acts of rebellion that are about as dangerous as a kitten in a cardboard box!

The Art of Strategically Timed "Technical Difficulties"

Sometimes, the universe decides to throw you a bone, like it's trying to help you out of the mess you've made. How generous of it! Let's say, your boss, who clearly thinks they're the king of the world, just tossed a last - minute demand for a presentation that's due in, what, five minutes? Your panic is rising faster than a soufflé, and trust me, it's not going to end well when it collapses. Oh, hold up! What if you could take this moment and turn it into a spectacular display of doing absolutely nothing? Sounds like your kind of talent! Welcome to the masterclass of perfectly executed "oops, my bad" moments.

See you're at your desk, desperately scrambling to create slides that would make even the most experienced PowerPoint guru question their life choices. Oh look, it's the classic escape route: "technical difficulties." What a shocker! With just a couple of keystrokes, your computer can freeze up like it's trying to win an Oscar for Best Supporting Actor in a horror flick. Bravo!

"Well, look who just discovered the concept of mistakes!" Oh great, my computer's off on a holiday while I'm here doing all the work. Must be nice to be a machine with better vacation days than I have! "Hold on, let me just give this thing a little wake - up call. It's clearly been napping too long." Oh look at you, acting like you've just discovered the secret to life by taking a moment to breathe. Go ahead, grab that snack; it's not like you were doing anything important anyway. Enjoy your little break while the world keeps spinning without you!

Let's get one thing straight: we're not suggesting you go full - on villain mode here. No one wants to be the office clown who trips over their own lies and ends up in a tangled mess of their own making. But hey, a perfectly timed "technical difficulty" can really work wonders in keeping those sky - high expectations in check, right? Just try to keep that stone - cold expression while you watch your poor friend twist in agony. And for the love of all things holy, keep the cackling to a minimum—no one needs to hear how happy you are in their misery.

The Automated "Out of Office" Reply: Your Shield and Sword

The automated "out of office" reply—a real champion of dodging responsibility like a pro. This little gem is like a glorified toolbox for your work life, pretending to be both a shield and a sword against the endless demands of those MFs.

Friday afternoon, and you're ready to escape for the weekend when your genius of a boss decides to grace you with an email demanding a report that was due yesterday. Instead of folding under pressure and burning the midnight oil, how about you whip up a snazzy OOO reply that says, "Thanks for your email! I'm currently out of the office, probably trying to figure out how to avoid work for just a little longer. I'll be back on Monday, so try not to miss me too much." Oh wow, look at you being all understanding! What a saint! Next, you'll be handing out medals for basic human decency.

Here's a little nugget of wisdom for you: the genius of the OOO reply is that it sends a clear message without having to scream, "Get lost!" It's like a cute little sign that screams, "I have a life beyond this cubicle, and good luck trying to change that."

Go ahead and unleash your inner Picasso with that OOO message! Just don't expect anyone to actually care. You might want to sprinkle in some humor, like, "I'm currently out of the office, probably lounging with a piña colada on a beach somewhere, living my best life while you're stuck here. I'll circle back to you after I've conquered my coconut." This not only lifts the vibe but also gives your buddy a little nudge that you're not their personal assistant on speed dial.

And if you really want to nail it, maybe set your OOO reply to kick in when you know your favorite nuisance is about to unleash a torrent of ridiculous requests. Good luck with that! It's like carrying around a rusty old knife, thinking it's a secret weapon, but really, it's just there to remind you how unprepared you are.

Setting Boundaries Without Confrontation

Now, let's look into the fine skill of establishing boundaries without turning it into a dramatic showdown. These folks just love a good mess, and they treat your free time like it's just another toy in their playroom to break and play with. But don't panic! With a sprinkle of charm, you can set those boundaries without causing a ruckus.

One clever trick is to wield your calendar like a trusty shield. Schedule some quality time for yourself—be it for lunch, a coffee break, or even a "very important meeting" with your couch. When your MF spots you in the zone, they tend to back off and let you enjoy your precious me - time. It's like hanging a "Do Not Disturb" sign and letting the universe do the talking for you!

And if they happen to ask why you're MIA, just flash a grin and say, "I have a prior commitment that's as unmovable as a stubborn mule!" This wonderfully ambiguous yet confidently delivered reply shuts down any chance of haggling. It's like declaring, "I'm swamped, and you better keep your hands to yourself!" while still looking all serious and stuff.

Another sneaky trick to set boundaries is to harness the magic of the "buffer." When your buddy approaches you with a totally outlandish request, you can reply with, "I'd be thrilled to assist with that!" But right now, I'm busy with whatever you thought was a big deal. Can we circle back to this once I've wrapped it up? This not only proves you're ready to lend a hand but also gives a cheeky nudge that you've got a few other things on your plate.

The Power of Humor

Finally, let's not overlook the sheer brilliance of laughter in your acts of defiance. When confronted with the ridiculousness of an MF's demands, a cleverly timed joke can lighten the mood and remind us all that we're just a bunch of humans trying to make sense of this wild ride called life.

For instance, if your MF throws yet another last - minute project your way, you could respond with a playful, "Wow, I didn't realize I signed up for the 'Last - Minute Miracle Worker' position! I'll give it my all to make a rabbit pop out of my hat!" This not only brightens the atmosphere but also cleverly points out just how absurd the whole thing is.

Ultimately, engaging in those quirky little acts of (mostly harmless) rebellion is all about striking that perfect balance between holding your ground and not losing your marbles. Whether it's through perfectly timed tech hiccups, automated "out of office" replies, or establishing boundaries with a giggle you can sail through the tricky seas of MF management with flair and some laughter.

As we finish our amusing peril through the quirky world of passive - aggressive resistance, let's pause to spotlight some essential principles that will help you stay on the sunny side of sanity while tiptoeing through the treacherous terrain of MFs. Just a friendly reminder, this isn't about plotting a coup or transforming your office into a backdrop for a wacky dystopian comedy. It's all about dodging disaster, sneaky tactics, and perhaps a sprinkle of playful troublemaking. Alright, let's jump right in and make a splash!

Professionalism First

First and foremost, let's clear the air: you are definitely not trying out for a part in the next installment of Office Space. As much as the idea of turning the office printer into a bonfire might tickle your fancy after a week of wrestling with your MF, let's try to keep our shenanigans on the right side of professionalism.

These tactics are all about staying alive, not going out in a blaze of glory. Your mission, should you choose to accept it, is to dance through the madness without earning a one - way ticket to the office's most unwanted list. So, maintain that sly wit, act all serious, and save those eye - rolls for your private collection. Imagine it as a game of chess, where each move is extremely important and you definitely want to dodge getting checkmated by your buddy's shenanigans.

When someone throws an outrageous request your way, instead of going off on a rant about how you can't pull rabbits out of hats, just take a deep breath and respond like the calm, cool cucumber you are. A perfectly timed grin and a little head bob can do wonders for keeping your professional vibe intact while still making your point loud and clear. Keep in mind, you're in it for the marathon, not the sprint, and being a pro is your secret weapon.

Keep It Plausible

Now, let's have a plausible chat! This isn't the moment to orchestrate a daring caper or launch a spectacular uprising fit for the silver screen. Your little rebellions should be sly enough to lift your spirits without raising any red flags at the office.

Consider your resistance tactics as a covert operation—like a ninja in a business suit, silently gliding through the office while keeping a low profile. The aim is to lighten your load, not to find yourself in a sticky situation with HR justifying why your "technical hiccups" always pop up during your MF's presentations.

So, when you're cooking up your subtly spicy replies, make sure they're seasoned with a touch of reality. A well - timed quip or a cleverly crafted email can pack just as much punch as a grand gesture, and they won't leave you sweating in the hot seat. Don't forget, a little finesse goes a long way.

Know When to Walk Away

Finally, let's tackle the big guy in the corner: sometimes, the most perfectly timed "out of office" reply can only go so far. If your workplace resembles a wacky sitcom, filled with laugh tracks and ridiculous plot twists, it might just be time to hatch a plan for your great escape!

Knowing when to take a hike is a key component of your slyly defiant toolkit! If Monday mornings have you feeling like a deflated balloon and you're ticking off the hours until the weekend like it's a countdown to freedom, it might just be a hint that your current surroundings aren't quite your cup of tea.

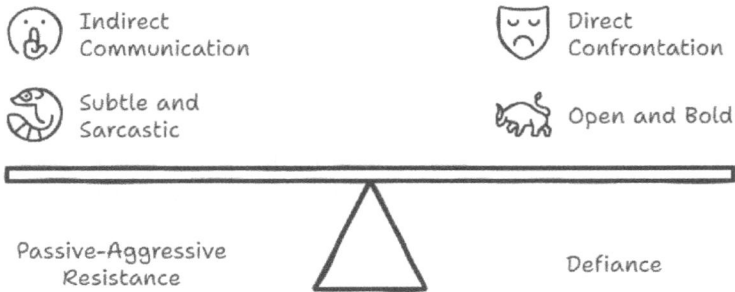

Choose your office battle strategy wisely.

Take a moment to weigh your options and see where you stand! Are the MFs in your life sucking the life out of your energy and creativity? Are you always tiptoeing around like you're on a fragile mission? If the answer is yes, it could be time to shake off that resume and start hunting for fresh opportunities.

Don't forget, you totally deserve to be in a workplace that appreciates your input and honors your limits. It's all about that respect, right? So, if the pandemonium gets a bit too wild, don't be shy to make your grand exit! After all, life is too short to be stuck in a job that feels like a rerun of a cringe - worthy sitcom.

Don't forget to hold onto these key principles—they're the real MVPs! Professionalism is the name of the game, plausibility is the ace up your sleeve, and knowing when to take a hike is key to staying in the right lane. With these guidelines tucked away, you'll be ready to sail through the choppy seas of MF management with flair, wit, and a sprinkle of mischief.

So, as you get started on your journey through the wilds of office politics, keep in mind: you hold the reins to resist, and you can do it all while maintaining your poise and grace!

$\smile\!\!\!\!\sim$

Chapter 11:
The Ultimate Revenge - Thriving Beyond Toxicity

BREAKING NEWS:

"The local employee successfully escapes the ninth circle of corporate hell! Sources say they were last seen speed - walking out of the building, carrying an overstuffed box of personal belongings. Former colleagues describe them as "finally free" and "glowing with the unbothered radiance of someone who will never have to explain the difference between urgent and fake urgent again."

Freedom. Sweet, glorious freedom. You did it. You escaped. You walked (or dramatically stormed) out of that toxic workplace and into a new life. No more passive - aggressive emails. No more last - minute "urgent" projects that could have been planned weeks ago. No more pretending to laugh at your boss's terrible jokes just to keep the peace.

And yet, why do you still feel like you got hit by a corporate truck?

Here's the thing about toxic workplaces—they don't just drain your energy while you're there. They leave behind a lingering effect, like a bad perfume that won't wash off. Even after you're gone, you might still catch yourself bracing for unnecessary feedback, over - explaining your decisions, or hesitating to take up meeting space. It's like a bad ex who still lives rent - free in your head, whispering doubts and making you question yourself.

But you know what's the good news: that voice? It's lying. You were never the problem. And now, it's time to shake off the baggage, reclaim your confidence, and get back to being the unstoppable professional you always were.

Reclaiming Your Professional Mojo

Let's get real—nothing wrecks your confidence quite like a toxic workplace. One day, you're a high - performing, self - assured professional, making things happen with the precision of a seasoned pro. The next? You're staring at your screen, second - guessing whether "Kind regards" sounds too formal or if "Best" makes you seem too casual. You start triple - checking emails for typos, even though you used to fire them off like a linguistic sharpshooter. That's the dark magic of bad management—it slowly erodes your confidence until you're questioning if you even deserve a keyboard.

News flash: you weren't the problem.

Step one to getting your mojo back? Take a moment to list your wins—every single one. That big project you nailed despite your manager's constant "just checking in" emails? Yep, that was you. The heroic client saved after someone else dropped the ball and somehow made it your problem? Also, you. Those insane deadlines that felt like they were set by someone who'd never seen a calendar? You crushed them like it was no big deal. Remember all those late - night emails where you were the one saving the day? You're not just competent—you're exceptional. You might have been gaslighted into thinking you were doing a bad job, but in reality, you were performing at a level that had your coworkers secretly wondering how you survived the madness.

The Employee Happiness Cycle: A Journey Through Disillusionment

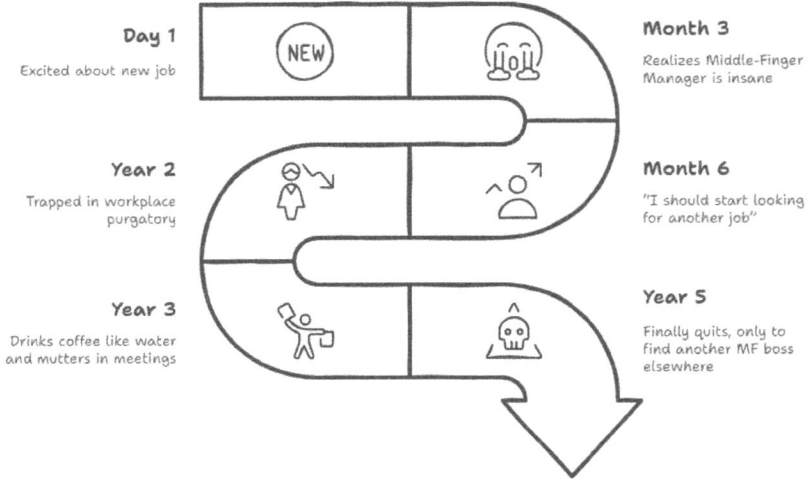

Day 1
Excited about new job

Month 3
Realizes Middle-Finger Manager is insane

Year 2
Trapped in workplace purgatory

Month 6
"I should start looking for another job"

Year 3
Drinks coffee like water and mutters in meetings

Year 5
Finally quits, only to find another MF boss elsewhere

Oh, and here's a bonus tip: Think of your toxic boss as an unintentional personal trainer. Sure, their nonsense drained every last ounce of your will to live, but guess what? It made you stronger. You managed impossible deadlines that felt like the universe had conspired to make you fail. You survived ridiculous last - minute changes and impossible deadlines (which they "forgot" to tell you about), ridiculous last - minute changes (because they "just had a thought"), and meetings that could have been a Slack message (but, of course, had to be scheduled as a video call... with cameras on).

If you survived that, you can survive anything. I mean, you're basically a warrior at this point. In a way, your toxic boss has been the villain in your origin story. Think of them as Lex Luthor, creating a Superman out of you without even realizing it. You're stronger, faster, and more resilient. You've conquered nonsense like a true hero, and now you're practically invincible. Your professional mojo? Untouchable. So go ahead, dust off your cape—you've earned it.

Building Your Dream Job, Brick by Brick

Once you realize the problem was never you (and that MMFs in your old office were basically a stress - inducing NPC in the chaotic video game of your career), it's time to plan your next move. Maybe you're eyeing a job that actually values your time—one where "work - life balance" isn't just an empty phrase slapped onto the company website right next to a stock photo of suspiciously happy employees. Or maybe you're done with corporate nonsense altogether and ready to go full Beyoncé and build your own empire. Either way, this is your moment to take the reins and create something that aligns with your values—something that doesn't make you question your entire existence at 3 a.m. while staring at the ceiling.

Take Lisa, for example. She spent years trapped under the thumb of a micromanager who believed meetings about meetings were a badge of efficiency. You know the type—the kind who schedules a 45 - minute call just to "touch base" on an email you already sent with all the information.

After one too many "urgent" requests that weren't actually urgent, Anna had enough, Anna snapped. Not in a dramatic, flip - the - conference - table kind of way (although let's be honest, she thought about it), but in a "this company does not deserve another ounce of my energy" kind of way. So, she quit. But instead of jumping into another corporate nightmare, Anna built something better. She started her boutique marketing agency, where morning meetings were replaced with "brainstorming coffee hours" (translation: everyone shows up in pajamas, sips coffee, and for real gets work done). No more endless Slack messages demanding "quick updates." No more tracking work on fourteen different project management tools. And most importantly, no one passive - aggressively commented on how many quirky coffee mugs she owned. Now, stress levels have plummeted, creativity is soaring, and Anna actually enjoys Mondays—something she once thought was only possible for dogs and retirees.

This isn't just about escaping a toxic job—it's about designing a better professional life. Maybe for you, that means negotiating a role that respects work - life balance (instead of just pretending to). Perhaps it's launching your dream business, one where you call the shots and "urgent" only means "actual emergency" and not "boss forgot to do something, and now it's your problem." Or maybe it's simply making a vow to never sit through another meeting that could have been an email.

Whatever your next step is, thriving beyond toxicity means putting yourself back in the driver's seat. And this time? You're not taking detours through Dysfunction Junction ever again.

Outgrowing the Petty Need for Revenge

Your old MF realizing you're thriving is a chef's - kiss level of satisfaction when they're trapped in yet another soul - crushing budget meeting, listening to a 47 - slide PowerPoint on "Cost Efficiency Strategies" (aka why Karen from accounting can't have color ink anymore). What if: their inbox is overflowing dumpster fire; their stress level is teetering on a breakdown, and then – bam - your name pops up on LinkedIn.

"Exciting career update: Just landed my dream role at a company that actually values its employees!"

The comments are pouring in, the likes are stacking up, and there they are—slack - jawed, staring at their screen, wondering how the employee they once belittled is now absolutely killing it. Somewhere, deep in their corporate heart, they feel... something. Is it regret? Jealousy? Acid reflux from that third cup of burnt office coffee? We'll never know.

The point is: true success isn't about proving them wrong. It's about getting to a place where they don't even cross your mind anymore. The best revenge isn't some dramatic exit speech, a scathing Glassdoor review, or an elaborate revenge plot where you send them 200 "urgent" meeting invites at 4:59 p.m. on a Friday (tempting, though). No, the real win is waking up actually excited for work, thriving in an environment that appreciates your skills, and never again feeling your stomach drop at a "Can we chat?" email.

That said, nothing confuses a toxic manager more than seeing the employee they tried to break go on to absolutely dominate elsewhere. Picture this scenario: Your old boss, still clinging to their *outdated* management playbook (probably titled *Micromanagement & Mistrust: A Leadership Guide*), takes a break from needlessly hovering over their team's shoulders. They open Instagram during their "working lunch" (aka eating a sad, dry turkey sandwich while firing off passive - aggressive Slack messages). And there you are—grinning, holding a *Best Workplace* Award at your new company. The caption?

Thriving where creativity is celebrated, not suffocated.

Meanwhile, they're still wondering why the team mysteriously goes offline every time a "quick sync" is scheduled. And the best part? Your post has more engagement than their company's entire LinkedIn presence.

Then come the run - ins. Maybe you bump into an old coworker at a coffee shop, and after some polite small talk, they drop, *"Yeah... things haven't been the same since you left. Actually, we just had another round of resignations."* You nod sympathetically, but inside? You're moonwalking with joy.

Or maybe - just maybe - you get that message. You know the one.

"Hey, hope you're doing well! We'd love to catch up. Things have changed around here, and we think you'd be a great fit to return!"

Oh, have they changed? *Really?* Did they finally outlaw the 6 a.m. "team - building" meetings? Did they throw away the "low - key toxic" office culture in favor of actual work - life balance? Did they finally grasp that "ASAP" doesn't mean dropping everything, neglecting hydration, and ignoring basic human needs?

The reality is by the time they realize how valuable you were, you're already *too far ahead* to care. You've moved on, leveled up, and built something better—whether it's a job where your talents are actually recognized, a business where *you* call the shots, or simply a work - life balance that doesn't involve waking up in a cold sweat from a nightmare about unread Slack messages.

When Your Old Job Realizes You Were Right All Along

You've been gone for a while now—thriving, glowing, and no longer haunted by the sound of MFs clearing their throat behind you. You've settled into your new job, where leadership values work - life balance, and "urgent" means real urgency, not just a manager's lack of planning. Life is good.

Then, one day, you hear the news: Your old company is adopting policies suspiciously similar to your new workplace. The same MFs that once rolled their eyes at the idea of flexible schedules and sustainable workloads are now rolling out a "proudly introduced" initiative for remote work and better time - off policies. The same MF leadership that used to micromanage lunch breaks is now "valuing work - life balance" and encouraging employees to set boundaries.

Oh, So Now Employee Happiness Matters?

For years, they ignored the warning signs—high turnover, plummeting morale, and the collective sigh of exhaustion every time a "quick sync" meeting appeared on the calendar. But after losing too many employees (and maybe a few clients), the company has undergone a sudden change of heart.

Now, flexible work schedules are a core part of company culture. Leaving at 5 PM is no longer a reason for judgment—it's encouraged. Leadership has replaced their "hustle harder" mentality with words like balance, mental health, and sustainable productivity.

It's almost impressive. Almost. Then, the cherry on top: you hear they had to hire two people to replace you.

Of course, they did.

Because while they were busy undervaluing your contributions, expecting you to juggle five different roles, and treating burnout like a badge of honor, they somehow forgot that you were holding everything together. Now, in your absence, they've realized that all that extra work didn't just magically do itself.

Even with two new hires, things aren't running as smoothly. Systems you streamlined are now tangled, deadlines are slipping, and the effortless way you kept everything on track is now glaringly absent.

And you? You're over here, flourishing in an environment that values you.

The Ultimate Mic Drop

Moral of the Story? Never let a toxic workplace convince you that you're not good enough. Because chances are, you weren't just good—you were essential. You carried more than you ever got credit for, and now that you're gone, they're scrambling to fill the void you left behind. But by the time they realize it, you'll be too busy thriving to even notice. In fact, you'll be building something much better—something that celebrates your worth and lets you work on your terms.

The real win isn't an overdue apology or a regret - filled email begging you to return. It's never needing one in the first place. It's waking up excited for work, knowing your talents are valued, and building a life where their opinions no longer hold weight. It's living in a reality where you're no longer the unsung hero but the main character, and the supporting cast is nothing but people who see you for exactly who you are—extraordinary.

And that? That's the ultimate mic drop—the kind you don't even have to stick around to hear. You walk away, head high, knowing your

⌣◯

Chapter 12:
Company Picnics and Team Building:
A Buffet of Awkwardness and Forced Fun

You must get the idea, company picnics and team - building exercises—the two - headed hydra of corporate camaraderie. Supposedly designed to foster teamwork, boost morale, and create lasting bonds, but in reality? They're just opportunities to make everyone as uncomfortable as possible outside the relative safety of their cubicles. If you've ever spent a sunny Saturday dodging your boss's terrible jokes while holding a soggy paper plate of potato salad, you know exactly what I mean.

The Company Picnic: Where Joy Goes to Die

Let's start with the classic company picnic, a day on which you're expected to trade your weekend plans for an awkward gathering at some park with questionable bathroom facilities. The email invite always promises *"fun for the whole family!"* as if dragging your kids to watch you suck up to your boss counts as fun.

What they don't tell you is that the *real* agenda of the picnic is to make you pretend you are part of a big, happy corporate family. Never mind the layoffs last quarter or the fact that your boss couldn't pick you out of a lineup. Today, you're all "one team," bonding over grilled hot dogs and warm soda.

Highlights of every company picnic include:

- **The Grill master Showdown:** Watching two middle managers passive - aggressively fight over who's the "real grill expert" while everyone pretends not to notice the flames getting dangerously high.

- **The Awkward Games:** Sack races and tug - of - war might sound fun until you're paired with Dave from accounting, who somehow turns a three - legged race into an Olympic event.

- **The Forced Mingling:** Your boss insists on making small talk with everyone, which means you'll spend ten minutes nodding politely as they overshare about their recent root canal.

- **The Talent Show:** Because nothing says "teamwork" like watching your coworker do a painful karaoke rendition of "Livin' on a Prayer" while everyone secretly records it for Instagram.

Team - Building Exercises: Torture in the Name of Morale

If company picnics are the appetizer, team - building exercises are the main course—a steaming pile of nonsense served with a side of humiliation. These activities are allegedly designed to bring coworkers closer together, but in practice, they're just elaborate ways to waste everyone's time. Instead of fostering teamwork, they create new reasons to resent each other—like being forced to do trust falls with people who won't even hold the elevator for you, watching your manager take a "friendly" competition way too seriously, or participating in a group challenge where the loudest person steamrolls every idea before disappearing when actual work needs to be done. And let's not forget the grand finale: a motivational speech from an executive who hasn't spoken to a non - managerial employee in years but now suddenly cares about "team synergy."

They claim these exercises boost morale, but all they really do is expose just how dysfunctional the workplace truly is and prove who's best at faking enthusiasm while quietly plotting their escape.

Classic team - building hits include:

- **The Trust Fall:** Nothing says "I value you as a colleague," like trusting Karen from HR to catch you while she's checking her email.

- **Escape Rooms:** Because nothing fosters cooperation like being locked in a tiny room with coworkers who can't agree on where to order lunch.

- **The Marshmallow Challenge:** An exercise in building towers out of spaghetti and marshmallows, which inevitably ends with someone yelling, "We're engineers, damn it, we should be good at this!"

- **Role - Playing Scenarios:** Pretending to be a customer service rep while your boss pretends to be an angry client isn't team building— it's just reliving your daily work nightmare in HD.

Why Companies Love These Events?

Let's be real: the only reason companies organize picnics and team - building events is to check a box that says, "Look, we care about our employees!" It's cheaper than raises and easier than addressing actual workplace issues. Plus, nothing distracts from a toxic culture quite like making everyone play charades.

For Middle - Finger Managers, these events are pure gold. They get to walk around pretending to be approachable while subtly reminding everyone who's in charge. "Oh, you didn't win the scavenger hunt? Well, maybe if you applied that same energy to your work..." And just like that, a day of "fun" becomes yet another tool for control and passive - aggressive commentary.

The Dreaded Icebreakers

No team - building session is complete without icebreakers, those cringe - inducing questions that make you long for the sweet release of the office fire alarm. Questions like:

- "If you were a tree, what kind would you be and why?"

- "What's your spirit animal?"

- "Tell us something no one here knows about you."

What no one mentions is that the only thing these icebreakers break is your will to live. No one cares that Janet from payroll once won a pie - eating contest, and Janet doesn't care that you've seen every episode of *The Office*. We're all just trying to survive until the coffee break.

The Unspoken Rules of Participation

Rule number one: You have to look like you're having fun, even if you're dying inside. Nothing will get you labeled as "not a team player" faster than refusing to participate in the human knot exercise or standing on the sidelines with your arms crossed like you have something better to do (which, let's be honest, you absolutely do). Even if you're awkwardly flailing through a three - legged race, you better slap on a smile and *pretend* you're enjoying yourself. Bonus points if you throw in a forced laugh at your manager's terrible joke—HR loves that.

Rule number two: Never outshine your boss. If your MF is on the opposing tug - of - war team, let them win. Their ego depends on it. Accidentally pulling a little too hard and watching your boss face - plant into the dirt might be hilarious, but it's also a one - way ticket to being mysteriously passed over for that promotion. The same rule applies to any competitive event—if your manager is in a company trivia match, suddenly develop amnesia. If they're manning the grill, nod approvingly even as you bite into what feels like a charcoal briquette. And if they're running in a relay race, well, now's the perfect time to clutch your hamstring and dramatically bow out. Just because you're off the clock doesn't mean office politics take a break.

Navigating Office Team-Building Events

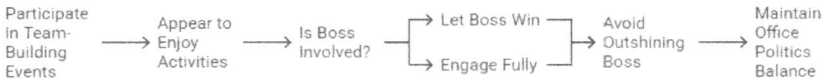

```
Participate              Appear to              Is Boss        ┌→ Let Boss Win ┐   Avoid          Maintain
in Team-         ───→    Enjoy          ───→    Involved?  ┤                    ├→ Outshining  ───→ Office
Building                 Activities                        └→ Engage Fully  ┘   Boss            Politics
Events                                                                                          Balance
```

How to Survive and Thrive

If you're stuck at one of these events, here are some tips for making it through without losing your sanity:

- **Perfect the Art of the Strategic Disappearance** – Find a moment when the spotlight isn't on you and casually fade into the background. Bonus points if you leave just before they start forcing people into a conga line.

- **Bring an Escape Plan** – Blame a "prior commitment" (real or fake). If questioned, use vague phrases like "family thing" or "important appointment." No one needs details.

- **Adopt the 'Enthusiastic but Unavailable' Approach** – Smile, nod, and claim you'd *love* to join the tug - of - war, but sadly, your knee/back/entire soul just isn't up for it.

- **Find the Snack Table and Stay There** – A plate of food in your hand at all times means fewer people trying to engage you in awkward small talk.

- **Buddy System:** Find a coworker who hates these events as much as you do and stick together. Misery loves company.

- **Set Boundaries:** If someone suggests karaoke, fake laryngitis. Trust me, it's worth it.

The "Fun" Awards Ceremony

No company event is complete without a forced, half - hearted awards ceremony where the same five people get recognized for things that don't matter. No one cares, yet somehow, we all clap as if our promotions depend on it. HR insists this is about "employee appreciation," but let's be honest—it's just another way to pad the event schedule so no one leaves early.

- **The "Most Enthusiastic" Award:** Given to the one person who actually enjoys these events (there's always one). This is the coworker who arrives *early*, voluntarily leads the group warm - up, and somehow thinks an egg - and - spoon race is a defining moment of corporate unity. They cheer a little too hard during tug - of - war, have face paint from the morning's "fun stations," and will tell *anyone* who will listen how much they "love company culture." They accept the award with genuine pride, beaming as if they just won an Oscar. Meanwhile, everyone else is exchanging looks that say, "How do we vote them off the island?"

- **The "Best Team Player" Award:** A thinly veiled reminder that the company expects you to keep carrying your lazy coworkers. This goes to the poor soul who stayed late to clean up, helped organize the scavenger hunt, and high - fived every single participant—even the ones who were actively trying to avoid human interaction. It's HR's way of saying, "Thanks for doing extra work for free! Now do it again next year." The worst part? This award comes with exactly **zero** perks. No bonus, no extra PTO—just an insincere round of applause and a cheap certificate that will live in a desk drawer until their next job interview.

- **The "Most Likely to Take One for the Team" Award:** Aka the poor soul who got *roped* into organizing this disaster. They didn't volunteer—oh no, they were *voluntold*. They spent weeks drowning in emails about catering, arguing with finance over a "strict budget," and politely nodding through middle management's "helpful suggestions" (read: unnecessary micromanaging). By the time they accept this award, they are a broken human being, holding back tears as they fake a smile and clutch a gift card to a restaurant they will never visit. Next year? They will *mysteriously* be "unavailable" when HR starts recruiting.

- **The Participation Trophies:** Because nothing says "we appreciate you" like a laminated certificate for "Best Effort in Sack Racing." These go to everyone HR is afraid of leaving out—think the guy who tripped over his own feet in the relay race, the intern who barely showed up, and the senior exec who *graciously* agreed to attend for five minutes before "an important call." But do you know the ultimate insult? You're expected to *act grateful* while HR takes a group photo of all the "winners." Congratulations, you now have a meaningless piece of paper to shove in a drawer until your next office purge.

The Real Takeaway

At the end of the day, company picnics and team - building exercises aren't about you—they're about appearances. They're about giving MFs another opportunity to assert dominance while pretending to care about employee morale. But here's the thing: you don't have to buy into the charade. Play the game, grab some free snacks, and remember that at least you'll get a good story out of it.

So, the next time you're handed a pair of potato sacks and told to "bond with your team," just smile, nod, and remind yourself: this, too, shall pass. And if all else fails, there's always the potato salad.

Post - Picnic Regrets

The event might be over, but the aftermath is just beginning. By Monday morning, your inbox will feature an HR email titled *"Great Times at the Company Picnic!* —a collection of embarrassing candids, including one of you mid - bite into a questionable hot dog. The office gossip mill will be in full swing, dissecting who got too drunk, who took the sack race *way* too seriously, and which two coworkers mysteriously disappeared together. Then there's the office's resident MF cheerleader, relentlessly hyping up the picnic as *the best event ever* while trapping you in the break room—forcing you to smile and nod as you mentally replay every awkward interaction you'd rather forget.

And finally, the cold reality sets in—your boss is still a micromanager, HR is still ignoring your emails, and the so - called *team bonding* vanished the moment everyone clocked in. The only lasting souvenir? A shared drive full of photos you wish didn't exist.

∽◯

Chapter 13:
Employee Reviews and HR: The Theater of the Absurd

The employee review process—corporate America's annual ritual of judgment and survival. A time - honored tradition where your worth as a human being is boiled down to a form with boxes to tick and phrases like *needs improvement* or *exceeds expectations.* And if that doesn't make you want to do a cartwheel into traffic, let's throw in the Human Resources Department, the self - proclaimed *neutral third party* that's about as neutral as a referee who moonlights for the opposing team.

Employee Reviews: The Farce Begins

Let's start with the obvious: the employee review is not about you. Oh, sure, they'll tell you it's an opportunity to *celebrate your achievements* and *identify growth areas,* but let's be real—it's an exercise in covering the company's butt. What if they need to fire you later? Well, they need a nice paper trail to justify it. That glowing review from last year? Yeah, forget that. This year, your "collaboration skills" are suddenly *under review.*

The format is always the same:

- **Step 1:** You fill out a self - assessment where you're supposed to "evaluate" yourself. This is a trap. If you rate yourself too high, you're arrogant. Too low? You lack confidence. Either way, you lose.

- **Step 2:** Your manager fills out their assessment, which is usually cobbled together 15 minutes before your meeting using a template they downloaded off the internet.

- **Step 3:** You sit through the meeting, where you're told what you already know: that you're doing fine, but not *fine enough* for a raise or promotion.

And let's not forget the feedback, which falls into two categories:

- **The Vague Compliment:** "You've been a valuable asset to the team." Translation: "I don't really know what you do here, but I'm obligated to say something nice."

- **The Corporate Critique:** "We'd like to see you take more initiative." Translation: "Do your job AND your boss's job, but for the same pay."

HR: The Guardians of Mediocrity

Now, let's talk about Human Resources—the department that's supposed to advocate for employees but mostly just exists to protect the company from lawsuits. HR loves to position itself as your ally, but the second you bring them an actual problem, they'll stare at you like you've just confessed to robbing a bank.

Here's a fun fact: HR is not your friend. Their job is to smile, nod, and file away your complaints in a folder labeled *Ignore Until Further Notice.*

Let's look at their greatest hits:

- **The "Open Door Policy" Lie:** HR claims you can "speak freely," but if you actually take them up on it, you'll soon find yourself on the receiving end of "constructive feedback" about your *attitude.*

- **The Investigation Black Hole:** You report something serious, and HR assures you they'll "look into it." Three months later, you follow up, and they've "escalated it to the appropriate channels," which is corporate - speak for "we're hoping you forget about this."

The Legendary: HR Wellness Webinar

HR loves to pretend they care, and nothing proves this more than their half - hearted attempts at "employee wellness." Their idea of support is less about *actual* change and more about sending you an email with a stock photo of a woman doing yoga and the subject line: *"Prioritize Your Mental Health!"* Meanwhile, your workload has doubled, your boss treats PTO like a personal betrayal, and the office coffee tastes like burnt regret—but sure, let's all take a deep breath and pretend that fixes everything.

But wait—there's more! They'll also offer *"stress relief"* activities like a mandatory meditation session during lunch (because nothing says relaxation like being forced to close your eyes and "breathe deeply" while Karen from accounting passive - aggressively taps her watch). Or maybe they'll set up a *self - care station*—a sad table with a coloring book, a single stress ball, and stale granola bars.

Need *real* support? A lighter workload? Better benefits? Fair pay? Oh no, HR doesn't *do* solutions. But they will send you an article about the benefits of journaling—as if writing *"I hate my job"* 50 times in a notebook will somehow fix your crushing burnout.

HR's solution to burnout isn't reducing workloads or hiring more staff—it's forcing you to attend a *very important* wellness webinar that achieves absolutely nothing except wasting an hour of your life. These gems include:

- **Mindfulness in the Workplace**: Because nothing soothes crushing deadlines like being told to "breathe deeply" while an overdue project looms over your shoulder.

- **Work - Life Balance: Finding Time for You**: A PowerPoint presentation delivered by someone who emailed you at 11 PM.

- **The Power of Positivity**: A session where they basically tell you to stop whining and smile more, because apparently, *toxic positivity* is a business strategy now.

The Great PTO Guilt Trip

HR loves to preach about *work - life balance*, but the second you try actually to have a life, you're met with the kind of resistance usually reserved for top - secret government files. You're technically *allowed* to take PTO— but much like the emergency exit row on a plane, using it comes with unspoken consequences.

The moment you submit your request, the passive - aggressive comments start rolling in:

- **The Thinly Veiled Jealousy:**

"Oh, you're taking time off? Must be nice! Guess we'll just have to survive without you."

Translation: We will absolutely make you pay for this later.

- **The Guilt Trip Special:**

"Are you sure this is the best time? The team is really busy right now..." As if there's *ever* a time when work isn't busy. You could request time off during a global office blackout, and they'd still claim there's too much going on.

- **The Classic Excuse:**

"We don't have the coverage."

Yes, because the entire business model apparently collapses the second you step away. Maybe, just maybe, that sounds like a *management problem* and not a *you* problem?

And if you actually dare to take time off? Prepare to spend the days leading up to it frantically tying loose ends while everyone passive - aggressively reminds you how much *your absence* will be felt. Then, when you finally get away, you'll still get "just one quick email" that somehow requires a two - hour response.

But the *real* punishment happens when you return. You walk back into the office only to find an inbox overflowing with *URGENT!!!* Emails that *somehow* no one else could answer, a pile of work that multiplied like rabbits in your absence and that one coworker who "covered" for you acting like they single - handedly ran the company while you were gone. And don't forget the meeting where you're expected to be 100% caught up within five minutes of sitting down.

HR claims PTO is encouraged, but the unwritten rule is clear: *taking a vacation is fine—just be prepared to suffer for it when you return.*

Performance Improvement Plans: The Kiss of Death

If you've ever been slapped with a Performance Improvement Plan, aka PIP, you'd know it's less about improving and more about planning your exit. HR frames it as a chance to "work collaboratively on areas of growth," but it's really just a checklist of reasons to fire you when you inevitably fail to meet their impossible standards.

Here's how it works:

- **Step 1:** They set "goals" for you that require the superpowers of a Marvel character.

- **Step 2:** They offer "support," which consists of vague advice like "communicate better" or "show more initiative."

- **Step 3:** They watch you flounder and then smugly conclude that you're just not a "good fit."

The PIP Process Pyramid

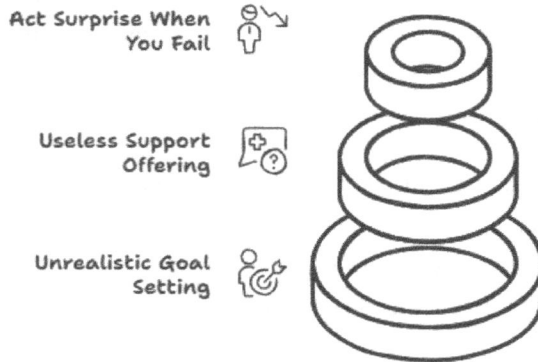

Act Surprise When You Fail

Useless Support Offering

Unrealistic Goal Setting

The Annual Review Dance

Let's not forget the true pièce de résistance of the employee review process: the annual review meeting. This is where you and your manager sit down for a painfully awkward conversation that's supposed to *motivate* you but mostly just makes you want to drink heavily.

Your manager will start with a compliment: "You've done great work this year." Then comes the pivot: "But we'd like to see you take things to the next level." This is corporate code for, "We need you to work harder for the same paycheck."

Then comes the most insulting part: the "merit increase." If you're lucky, you'll get a 2% raise—barely enough to cover inflation but just enough for them to say they gave you something.

How to Survive the Madness

Here's your survival guide:

- **Play the Game, but Play It Better:** Nod thoughtfully, throw in a few corporate buzzwords ("synergy," "proactive mindset," "leveraging cross - functional collaboration"), and let them think you care. Bonus points if you can get your manager to quote *your* nonsense back to you in the next review.

- **Master the Art of Strategic Incompetence:** If you're suddenly tasked with "stepping up," pretend to try but do it just badly enough that they never ask again. "Oh, you wanted *me* to lead the project? Gosh, I thought Sheila was handling that. My mistake!"

- **Create Your Own Paper Trail:** Keep an email folder labeled "Covering My Ass." Document every contribution, idea, and "collaborative effort" (aka when your boss steals your work) so that when review season rolls around, you have receipts.

- **Weaponize Their Own Feedback Against Them:** If they say, "We'd like to see you take more initiative," respond with, "Great, I'd love to lead—can we discuss a title change and salary adjustment?" Watch them backpedal so fast that they leave skid marks.

- **Use HR's Nonsense Against Them:** When HR feeds you the "we're here to support you" line, test it. Ask for a salary review. Request a four - day workweek. See how quickly their smiles evaporate.

The Takeaway

Employee reviews and HR are like a bad marriage—stuck together out of obligation, but nobody's happy. Reviews exist to keep you in line, and HR is there to ensure you don't sue when they inevitably fail to meet your needs. The whole process is a performance with you as the reluctant main character in a play you never auditioned for.

And what's your grand prize after all the corporate hoop jumping? A crisp 2% raise (before taxes) and a pat on the back that somehow manages to feel both insincere and insulting. Meanwhile, your boss takes credit for your work, HR reminds you how "lucky" you are to be employed, and the cycle resets for another year.

But here's the secret they don't want you to know: You're worth more than a box - ticking exercise or a half - hearted compliment in a performance review. So, take the feedback, file it under *meh*, and keep doing what you do best—surviving and thriving despite their best efforts to make you feel otherwise.

Because next year? Same forms. Same buzzwords. Same soul - crushing routine. And just like that, the *Theater of the Absurd* renews for another season—starring you, the overworked, underpaid lead who deserves an Oscar for pretending to care.

Conclusion:
The Future of Work and Leadership

As we tie a bow on this harrowing excursion through the topsy - turvy world of MF, let's pause to chuckle at the sheer ridiculousness of it all. We've spun accounts of praise pilferers, micromanagement maestros, and the mysteriously absent "good boss" who appears to be on an endless getaway. But don't be chicken! This isn't merely a compilation of horror reports; it's a rallying cry for a workplace that emanates brighter—where MFs are as uncommon as a unicorn at a corporate meeting.

Changing Landscape of Leadership

The future of work is changing gears, and so are the hopes for leadership to steer the ship! Gone are the days when howling commands and ruling with an iron paw were seen as top - notch management tactics. Today's workforce is a real mixed bag, more connected than ever, and—let's face it—way less willing to put up with the MF shenanigans that have been hanging around offices for far too long.

So, what does this bold new universe have in store for us? Think about a workplace where leaders lift spirits instead of lowering them, where teamwork is the name of the game, and the only thing getting a close watch is the office coffee pot brewing up some good vibes. It's a bright outlook, but it also needs a sprinkle of self - awareness and a dash of readiness to shake things up!

1. Embrace Vulnerability

One of the most refreshing trends in leadership is the shift toward being open and unguarded. Absolutely, you caught that correctly! Leaders who can own up to their blunders and reveal their human side are more relatable and, if we may say, more effective. It's a real win - win situation! Keep in mind, nobody's keen on trailing a tin can that just rattles off business buzzwords! Instead, we want leaders who can say, "Hey, I tripped up, but let's untangle this knot together!" It's like a support group, but instead of crying over spilled milk, we're pouring out ideas and getting things done!

2. Foster Open Communication

If there's one thing we've gleaned from our case studies, it's that communication really unlocks the door to success! MFs flourish in settings where information is kept under wraps like a prized pie crust recipe! But in the future, we need to shatter those silos and fire some open chatter! Leaders' ought to cultivate environments where employees can freely express their thoughts, share their bright ideas, and, when the occasion calls for it, give a little nudge to those MFs! Consider it a workplace democracy—without the never - ending debates and those cringe - worthy handshakes!

3. Prioritize Employee Well - Being

Let's not beat around the bush: a cheerful worker is a productive worker! The future of work is calling for leaders to put their teams' well - being at the top of their to - do list! This means bending over backwards to offer flexible work arrangements, striking a balance between work and life, and serving up resources for mental health on a silver platter. After all, if your employees are feeling frazzled and fried, they won't be serving up their A - game at the table! So, let's trade in the "hustle culture" for a "healthy culture" and see the enchantment unfold.

4. Lead by Example

If you want to steer clear of becoming an MF yourself, it's essential to set the right course by leading with a shining example. This means being the values you want to see in your team, like a role model with a mission! If you're all about that collaboration life but are always MIA in your office, well, that's a bit of a mixed message, isn't it? Your team is ready to toe the line. So, get out there, roll up your sleeves, and lead the way like a true champ! Show your team how to rise to the occasion! It's like being the captain of a ship - if you're at the helm, everyone else will want to sail along on your adventure.

Real - Life Example: Laughing at Absurdity

While the future may seem a bit wobbly, one thing is crystal clear: the more we chuckle at the silliness of poor management, the more we're likely to build workplaces where everyone's input is truly appreciated! Consider the story of a company that opted to celebrate a "Bad Boss Day," allowing employees to dish out their most outrageous MF stories in a hilariously light - hearted atmosphere. It not only brewed a sense of togetherness among the team, but it also unlocked a treasure chest of discussions about what makes a leader shine!

By shining a light on the hilarity of their past experiences, employees were able to connect over shared frustrations and hatch some egg - cellent ideas for a more uplifting workplace culture. It was a real "feel - good" experience that reminded everyone they weren't "struggling" alone—and that "change" was definitely on the horizon!

Creating Workplaces Where Everyone's Contributions Shine (and No One Gets Flipped Off)

The workplace can occasionally resemble a three - ring circus, featuring clowns, acrobats, and that one brave soul who thinks they can tame the wild beasts (a.k.a. your boss). But it doesn't have to be like this, right? With a dash of creative ability and a pinch of wit, each of us can turn our workplaces into spots where everyone feels appreciated, respected, and—let's be honest—genuinely thrilled to show up!

The Recipe for a Positive Workplace Culture

Picture this: you're a chef in a chaotic kitchen, ready to cook up a scrumptious dish known as "Positive Workplace Culture." Here's the secret recipe for whipping up a batch of success:

A Pinch of Empathy

Begin with a big scoop of understanding, like it's ice cream on a hot day! This is the magical elixir that turns bland into grand. When leaders actually bother to see things from their employees' point of view, it turns the workplace into a cozy little hangout instead of a stuffy office. Imagine it as the chicken broth of workplace culture - absolutely vital for whipping up a deliciously chaotic stew.

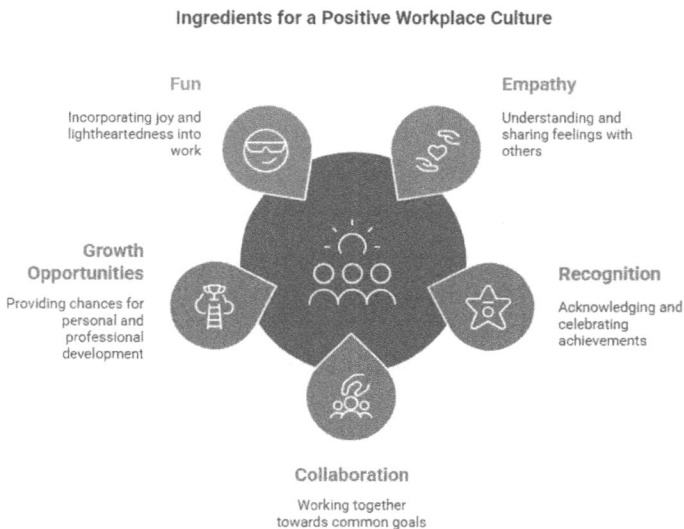

Ingredients for a Positive Workplace Culture

Fun
Incorporating joy and lightheartedness into work

Empathy
Understanding and sharing feelings with others

Growth Opportunities
Providing chances for personal and professional development

Recognition
Acknowledging and celebrating achievements

Collaboration
Working together towards common goals

A Dash of Recognition

Next, toss in an instant of applause! Who doesn't enjoy a solid pat on the back? Or if you're in the mood for some excitement, a high - five will do the trick! Throw a party for every little win, because who doesn't love a reason to celebrate? Keep that spirit soaring! It's like throwing confetti on a boring Tuesday—who wouldn't want a dash of delight in their day?

A Splash of Collaboration

Now, toss in a dash of teamwork magic! Get everyone to play nice and chat it up, and you'll see ideas pop like corks on New Year's Eve! When employees feel at ease tossing around ideas, it's like a potluck where everyone shows up with their A - game dish, and you just hope no one brings that weird jello salad! The more, the party - er!

A Generous Serving of Growth

Make sure to dish out some chances for growth, or you might just end up with a side of stagnation! Provide a hilarious mix of training, mentorship, and a roadmap to climb the career ladder without tripping over your own feet! This is the muscle - packed superstar of your cultural feast— absolutely important in making strong, capable employees who can tackle anything! When folks think they can level up, they're way more inclined to hang out and pitch in at the buffet of life.

A Side of Fun

At long last, throw in an extra pinch of hilarity! A workplace culture that's all about good vibes is one where giggles are a must, and employees can really cut loose! Whether it's game days, themed dress - up events, or spontaneous dance parties, an extra dose of silliness can turn any gathering into a lively bash! It's like the cherry on top of a sundae—everyone can't wait to dig in!

In this utopia, finding an MFs is like spotting a unicorn trying to bargain a deal in a boardroom. Instead, you have leaders who apply a little magic, lift spirits, and hand out empowerment like its candy at a parade. They totally get that a cheerful employee is a busy bee, and they're all in on composing a space where everyone can shine like a disco ball!

The Takeaway: It's Up to Us

Building a happy workplace isn't just a job for the big bosses; it's a group project, and everyone gets to pitch in! Every single person has a part to play in creating a space where what you bring to the table is appreciated and where respect is the VIP of the party. So, whether you're the head chef or just a sous - chef in the kitchen, grab these ingredients and whip up a culture that's a feast for everyone's enjoyment!

With just a bit of effort, a bucketful of guffaw, and a promise to have each other's backs, we can turn our workplaces into joyful jungles of positivity. Well, isn't that a mystery wrapped in an enigma? Who can say? Perhaps one day, we'll joke at the ridiculousness of middle - finger management, realizing we were part of establishing something genuinely unique.

You're Not Alone

First things first, let's tackle the big guy in the corner: if you've ever felt like you were the lone ranger battling an MF, take a deep breath and relax—you're definitely not alone in this wild ride! We've all found ourselves tiptoeing through the treacherous terrain of office politics, expertly dodging those passive - aggressive emails like they're ninja stars, all while attempting to keep our sanity from doing a dramatic exit stage left. It's like joining a club where the initiation fee is your dignity, and the only rule is to outlast the chaos!

Now, Imagine Selena, trapped in a job that seemed less like a career and more like a scene from a sitcom where the punchline never lands. Her MF was a wizard of wiggling words, and each day felt like a hilarious tug - of - war. But instead of letting it shatter her spirit like a piñata at a kid's birthday party, Selena decided to take action. She began chronicling her wild adventures, reaching out to her work buddies for backup, and eventually mustered the guts to ditch that dreadful place for good. Today, she's thriving in a job that values her contributions, and she often quips that her old MF is likely still wrestling with the office printer like it's a wild beast.

The Path Forward

Let's make a commitment to be the sort of leaders who encourage, empower, and inspire others around us as we go forward. Let's build workplaces where the drama queens are a thing of the past, and every employee feels like a superstar with a megaphone! It's time to toss those old management practices out the window and welcome a fresh era of leadership—one that puts empathy, teamwork, and a hearty laugh at the top of the list.

So, as you walk into your next meeting or look into your next project, keep in mind the wisdom gathered from the battlefield of experience. Whether you're the captain of the ship or just a trusty deckhand, you've got the magic wand to conjure up the future of work! Well, isn't that a mystery wrapped in an enigma? With a bit of titters and a hefty dose of love, we just might whip up a workplace revolution that has the MFs scratching their heads in utter bewilderment. After all, if we can flip the script on toxic management, we can turn our workplaces into stages where creativity takes center stage and everyone feels like a superstar.

The Role of Humor in Leadership

Let's not overlook the magic of laughter in the office. A perfectly placed punchline can clear the air quicker than a fire extinguisher at a cookout gone wrong. Leaders who can chuckle at their own quirks and the ridiculousness of office antics foster a vibe where employees can truly let their hair down. It's like wielding a ninja star against the pesky MFs of the universe. So, don't hesitate to toss in a dash of humor into your leadership approach.

Just keep in mind, there's a delicate balance between cracking jokes and falling flat—so watch your step!

In the future, let's throw a party for every little victory, even if it's just finding matching socks. Did someone finally perform a miracle on that printer that's been throwing tantrums for months? Host a tiny bash! Did a team member hit the jackpot with a genius idea during a brainstorming session? Give them a big ol' shout - out! Spotting achievements is like throwing a party for your brain, making everyone feel like they belong and giving them that extra nudge to keep hustling. And really, who can resist a good slice of cake?

The future of work is like a wild rollercoaster ride, where innovation is the ticket and taking risks is the thrilling loop - de - loop that everyone's cheering for! Some folks really know how to squash creativity by throwing a tantrum over failure, but in a universe where ideas are the real bucks, we should totally roll with the punches and laugh at our missteps! Get your team to unleash their wild imaginations, try out crazy ideas, and embrace the art of goofing up. After all, every great invention kicked off as a zany thought that someone had the guts to chase down.

Diversity isn't just a trendy phrase; it's the secret sauce for a workplace that actually works. The future of leadership is all about throwing a big welcome party where everyone gets a name tag and a warm fuzzy feeling. Let's make sure no one's left out in the cold! This means going on a treasure hunt for different viewpoints and making sure every voice gets its moment in the spotlight! When we welcome our quirks, we stumble upon a goldmine of creativity and innovation that can launch our organizations into the stratosphere.

⤺

The Corporate Circus: Bonus Details You Didn't Ask For

Glossary of Middle - Finger Management

Here's a glossary of **50 Middle - Finger Manager phrases**— translated into common - sense, sarcastic definitions in the signature C. V. Wooster style:

1. **"Circle back later."**

Translation: I have no intention of ever addressing this, but let's pretend we will.

Common Sense: Avoidance masquerading as strategy.

2. **"Run it up the flagpole."**

Translation: Let's suggest this ridiculous idea to someone higher up and hope they're too busy to reject it.

Common Sense: Blame delegation at its finest.

3. **"It will only take a minute."**

Translation: This will derail your entire day, but I don't care because I already outsourced thinking to you.

Common Sense: Multiply by 500.

4. "Think outside the box."

Translation: I need ideas but will shoot down anything remotely creative.

Common Sense: The box is a coffin, and you're in it.

5. "Let's not reinvent the wheel."

Translation: Let's copy what's been done a thousand times and call it innovative.

Common Sense: Fear of originality.

6. "Circle of trust"

Translation: A group I have already betrayed but still expect loyalty from.

Common Sense: Cult - adjacent vibes.

7. "Perception is reality."

Translation: Lie convincingly enough, and people will believe it.

Common Sense: Truth is irrelevant.

8. "Keep it on my radar."

Translation: I'm going to forget this exists in about five seconds.

Common Sense: Total dismissal with flair.

9. "We're a family here."

Translation: Expect to be underpaid, overworked, and guilt - tripped for not working weekends.

Common Sense: Dysfunction, but with birthday cakes.

10. "Take ownership."

Translation: I'm dumping this mess on you because I don't want to deal with it.

Common Sense: Unpaid managerial training.

11. "Low - hanging fruit."

Translation: Let's aim for the easiest, least innovative solution and call it a success.

Common Sense: Mediocrity rebranded.

12. "Give 110%"

Translation: Burn yourself out so I can look good at the next meeting.

Common Sense: Math wasn't their strong suit.

13. "This is a priority."

Translation: Everything else you're working on is now irrelevant. Drop it.

Common Sense: Panic management.

14. "We need to pivot."

Translation: We screwed up, but let's call it a strategic adjustment.

Common Sense: Corporate pirouette into chaos.

15. "Touch base."

Translation: I need to feel busy, so I'll interrupt you for no reason.

Common Sense: A pointless check - in.

16. "Let's drill down."

Translation: I need to micromanage this until it's completely ruined.

Common Sense: Dismantling something functional.

17. "Can you hop on a quick call?"

Translation: I'm too lazy to email.

Common Sense: Time vampire alert.

18. "Let's table this."

Translation: I hate your idea but don't want to argue about it right now.

Common Sense: Procrastination tactic.

19. "Win - win."

Translation: I win, and you get to stay employed.

Common Sense: A single winner wearing a double mask.

20. "Open - door policy."

Translation: Come talk to me, but only if it's flattering.

Common Sense: The door is imaginary.

21. "Let's take this offline."

Translation: This discussion is making me look bad, so let's bury it later.

Common Sense: Avoidance with a side of deflection.

22. "We need to create synergy."

Translation: Let's throw together a group of people and hope something productive happens.

Common Sense: Buzzword bingo.

23. "This is above my pay grade."

Translation: I could help, but I won't.

Common Sense: Excuse for indifference.

24. "Let's align."

Translation: Change your opinion to match mine.

Common Sense: Obedience, corporate - style.

25. "Leverage our strengths."

Translation: Let's exploit whoever is most competent.

Common Sense: Resource extraction.

26. "Do more with less."

Translation: Work harder with fewer resources so I can meet my budget goals.

Common Sense: Enjoy your burnout.

27. "We're not here to point fingers."

Translation: I'm 100% blaming you, but in a passive - aggressive way.

Common Sense: Finger - pointing in disguise.

28. "Let's keep this at a high level."

Translation: I don't understand the details, so let's avoid them.

Common Sense: Oversimplification.

29. "We're building the plane while flying it."

Translation: We have no idea what we're doing, but we're too far in to stop.

Common Sense: Disaster - in - progress.

30. "It's a marathon, not a sprint."

Translation: Prepare for never - ending misery.

Common Sense: Eternal exhaustion.

31. "Let's workshop this."

Translation: I have no solutions, but let's pretend brainstorming is progress.

Common Sense: Spinning wheels for fun.

32. "This isn't personal."

Translation: I'm about to make it very personal.

Common Sense: Gaslighting 101.

33. "Let's circle the wagons."

Translation: Let's defend our bad decisions together.

Common Sense: Groupthink shield.

34. "We need all hands on deck."

Translation: Panic mode - everyone, stop what you're doing and fix my problem.

Common Sense: Organizational freak - out.

35. "Let's cross that bridge when we get to it."

Translation: I'll ignore this problem until it's unavoidable.

Common Sense: Procrastinator's anthem.

36. "Keep me in the loop"

Translation: Do all the work and update me so I can take credit later.

Common Sense: Control with zero effort.

37. "Let's reframe the narrative."

Translation: Let's spin this disaster into something that sounds intentional.

Common Sense: PR Band - Aid.

38. "Let's park this idea."

Translation: Bury this and hope it dies quietly.

Common Sense: Corporate graveyard.

39. "Think of this as an opportunity."

Translation: I'm giving you a pile of extra work with no extra pay.

Common Sense: Exploitation spin.

40. "Take it to the next level."

Translation: Work harder without expecting a promotion.

Common Sense: Goalposts just moved.

41. "Let's create a roadmap."

Translation: Let's make an overly complicated plan we'll ignore.

Common Sense: Useless formality.

42. "We're streamlining operations."

Translation: Brace for layoffs.

Common Sense: Budget - slashing euphemism.

43. "This is a teachable moment."

Translation: I'm using your mistake to lecture everyone.

Common Sense: Public shaming.

44. "Let's touch on that."

Translation: Let's briefly acknowledge this issue without resolving it.

Common Sense: Lip service.

45. "We're setting the bar high."

Translation: Prepare for unrealistic expectations.

Common Sense: Unreachable goals incoming.

46. "This will be a quick meeting."

Translation: Cancel your lunch plans.

Common Sense: Time warp ahead.

47. "Let's empower the team."

Translation: I'm going to delegate everything and take credit for the results.

Common Sense: Fancy word for passing the buck.

48. "We're pivoting to a new focus."

Translation: Everything you worked on is now irrelevant. Start over.

Common Sense: Reinventing failure.

49. "This is just a soft ask."

Translation: Do this now, but I don't want to sound demanding.

Common Sense: Passive - aggressive orders.

50. "Let's put a pin in that."

Translation: I don't like your idea, but I'm too polite to say so.

Common Sense: Rejection with a smile.

Interactive Elements for Surviving Middle - Finger Managers: A Survival Guide

Welcome to the **Interactive Elements** section—a.k.a. your personal toolbox for navigating the circus of corporate absurdity led by your Middle - Finger Manager (MF). These activities aren't just for venting (though we're all for a good rant); they're also here to give you a sense of control, a dose of humor, and maybe even a fresh perspective on the madness of office life. Think of this as your sarcastic, stress - relieving companion to surviving the workplace without flipping your own metaphorical middle finger at the world.

Each activity is designed to help you laugh at the ridiculousness, analyze your situation, and maybe even feel a little less alone in the chaos. So, grab a pen, a donut, and your favorite beverage—let's turn that workplace misery into some much - needed comic relief!

1. Middle - Finger Bingo

Instructions: Create a bingo card with classic MF phrases like "circle back," "it's a great learning opportunity," and "we need to think outside the box." Bring it to your next meeting and silently check off squares as your MF spews nonsense.

Purpose: Adds a layer of entertainment to otherwise soul - crushing meetings.

2. The Toxic Workload Pie Chart

Instructions: Draw a pie chart dividing your time into categories like "actual work," "fixing the boss's mistakes," "attending pointless meetings," and "emotional recovery."

Purpose: Gain clarity on how much time you're wasting thanks to your MF.

3. Office Buzzword Counter

Instructions: Keep a tally of how often your boss says phrases like "synergy," "low - hanging fruit," or "thought leadership."

Purpose: Helps you quantify the absurdity and perhaps avoid snapping the next time "circle back" enters the chat.

4. Your MF's Spirit Animal Quiz

Instructions: Answer a series of sarcastic questions to discover if your MF is a Peacock (all show, no substance), a Hyena (loud and irritating), or a Sloth (slow - moving but equally annoying).

Purpose: Provides comic relief and a new way to describe your boss to friends.

5. The Blame Flowchart

Instructions: Follow this simple decision tree:

Did something go wrong? → Yes → Blame the employee.

Was it a success? → Yes → MF takes credit.

Purpose: Humorously highlights your MF's inability to take accountability.

6. Emotional Frustration Meter

Instructions: Rate your frustration daily on a scale from 1 to 10, with prompts like:

1: "Mild irritation, probably coffee - related."

10: "Ready to burn my ID badge and move to a yurt."

Purpose: Helps track your mental state while working under an MF.

7. The Venting Journal

Instructions: Use the prompt: "Dear Diary, today my boss did..." Fill in the blank with your wildest work woes.

Purpose: Let off steam without throwing your computer across the room.

8. MF Translator Tool

Instructions: Write down a phrase your MF uses and translate it into what they really mean.

Example: MF says, "This is a great team effort."

Translation: "I'm taking credit for your work."

Purpose: Adds clarity to corporate doublespeak.

9. The "Most Valuable Petty Tyrant" Award

Instructions: Create a fake certificate for your boss with categories like "Best Performance in Micromanaging" or "Most Passive - Aggressive Email Sent in an Hour."

Purpose: Sarcastic fun for after - work drinks.

10. Exit Strategy Checklist

Instructions: Create a checklist of steps to leave your job, like "polish LinkedIn profile," "network discreetly," and "practice resignation speech."

Purpose: Keep yourself focused on the light at the end of the tunnel.

11. Corporate Lingo Redecoration

Instructions: Redesign the "Mission Statement" poster in your office with more honest phrases like:

Original: "We value teamwork."

Updated: "We value blaming others for our mistakes."

Purpose: Inject humor into your workspace.

12. The Passive - Aggressive Email Template

Instructions: Write your own passive - aggressive emails to mirror your MF's tone.

Example: "Per my last email..." → Translation: "Why can't you read?"

Purpose: Fight sarcasm with sarcasm (but don't hit send!).

13. The Burnout Scale

Instructions: Gauge how close you are to total burnout by answering questions like: "How often do you daydream about hammocks?" or "Do you fantasize about being fired just to get a break?"

Purpose: Identify burnout before it consumes you.

14. The Perpetual Sidekick Quiz

Instructions: Determine how often your boss makes you the Robin to their Batman, despite doing all the work.

Purpose: Helps you pinpoint why you're frustrated.

15. The Doormat Self - Test

Instructions: Assess how often you're "volunteered" for extra tasks with no reward.

Purpose: Helps you recognize toxic patterns.

16. Buzzword Mad Libs

Instructions: Create ridiculous sentences using buzzwords from your office.

Example: "Let's synergize the paradigm shift while leveraging innovative ecosystems."

Purpose: Laughter as a coping mechanism.

17. Stress - Eating Tracker

Instructions: Document how often your MF drives you to donuts, chips, or chocolate.

Purpose: Self - awareness is the first step to recovery.

18. The Compliment Log

Instructions: Track how often your MF gives compliments and rank them for sincerity.

Purpose: A reminder that praise is not their strong suit.

19. MF Excuse Generator

Instructions: Write down excuses your MF uses to avoid accountability.

Example: "I didn't know about the deadline!"

Purpose: Catalog the ridiculousness.

20. Recognition Fantasy Board

Instructions: Imagine what real recognition would look like.

Purpose: A reminder that you deserve better.

21. The Petty Olympics

Instructions: Rank your MF's petty behaviors on a scale of 1 to gold medal.

Purpose: Fun with co - workers.

22. Workplace Pet Peeves List

Instructions: Write out all your workplace pet peeves—bonus points if your MF ticks every box.

Purpose: Venting therapy.

23. MF Drinking Game

Instructions: (For after hours) Take a sip whenever your MF says their signature phrase or sends an unnecessary email.

Purpose: Bonding over shared frustrations.

24. Meeting Survival Checklist

Instructions: Create a checklist for staying awake in meetings: "Doodle sarcastic comics.", "Write your grocery list." Etc.

Purpose: Avoid zoning out.

25. MF Fantasy Response Bank

Instructions: Write out sarcastic responses you wish you could say to your MF but never will.

Purpose: Catharsis without consequences.

ⱺ

How to Know If You're an MF: A Quick Self - Check Exercise

Let's start with the obvious: if you're reading this chapter, chances are you've had a sneaking suspicion that you might just be one of them—a Middle - Finger Manager (MF for short). Or maybe someone anonymously slipped this book onto your desk, and you're starting to wonder why. Either way, congratulations! Recognizing you have a problem is the first step on the road to recovery. And trust me, your employees are rooting for you—mostly because they've already Googled "resignation letter templates" and are just waiting for the right moment to hit send.

But don't worry. Redemption is possible! It's not easy, of course. Changing your Middle - Finger ways require effort, self - awareness, and the ability to resist the urge to micromanage the color - coded pens in the supply closet. But if you're willing to try, you can transform from a soul - crushing tyrant into the kind of boss who inspires their team, gets results, and doesn't cause their employees to cry in the office bathroom.

Before we dive into strategies for change, let's figure out how deep into Middle - Finger territory you are. Here's a simple test. Rate yourself on a scale of 1 to 10 for each statement below, with 1 being "never" and 10 being "Oh no, that's me every Monday."

1. Do you feel the need to check every single email your team sends before it goes out?

2. When something goes wrong, is your first instinct to find someone to blame?

3. Have you ever taken credit for an idea that wasn't yours? (Be honest, Karen.)

4. Do your employees visibly flinch when you say, "Can I see you in my office for a moment?"

5. Are you allergic to giving compliments unless they're backhanded?

6. Do you schedule meetings that could have been emails? (Extra points if they're at 8 a.m.)

7. Is your "constructive feedback" basically a long - winded critique with zero actionable advice?

8. Do you think burnout is a sign of weakness?

9. Have you ever uttered the phrase, "It'll only take a minute," when assigning a task that takes hours?

10. When your team succeeds, do you celebrate *yourself* more than the people who made it happen?

Now, tally up your score.

0–20: Congratulations, you are human! You've got some quirks, but you're not a MF.

21–50: Uh - oh. You're teetering on the edge. There's hope, but you've got work to do.

51–100: Welcome to MF Headquarters. Your employees probably have a dartboard with your face on it. It's time for an intervention.

Why Change?

Now that you've identified where you stand on the MF scale, let's talk about why you should care. Changing your ways isn't just about making your employees' lives less miserable (though that's a nice bonus). It's also about your growth, reputation, and long - term success. Here's what's in it for you:

1. **Happier Employees = Better Results.**

It is almost the end of the book, and you must have gotten the idea where this one is going. Believe it or not, employees who aren't terrified of their boss tend to perform better. Shocking, right?

Happy workers are productive workers, and productive workers make *you* look good.

2. **Less Turnover, Fewer Headaches.**

Every time an employee quits because of you, it costs your company money—and it costs you time. Do you really want to spend half your life onboarding new hires because you can't stop being a jerk?

3. **Reputation Matters.**

Word gets around. If you're an MF, people will talk—and not in a good way. Fixing your image now could save your career down the line.

4. **Your Sanity.**

Let's face it: being an MF is exhausting. The constant need to micromanage, control, and blame is draining. Wouldn't it be nice to, I don't know, trust your team for once?

Strategies for Leaving the Middle - Finger Behind

Here are some actionable steps to start your transformation from MF to magnificent boss:

1. **Shut Up and Listen.**

I know, it's hard. But try it. The next time your team is discussing a project, resist the urge to dominate the conversation. Just listen. You might learn something.

2. **Give Credit Where It's Due.**

If someone on your team has a great idea, acknowledge it—publicly. Say, "That's a fantastic suggestion, Sarah," instead of, "I've been thinking about this for a while, and Sarah reminded me..."

3. **Stop Micromanaging.**

Repeat after me: "I don't need to control every detail." Trust your team to do their jobs. If they mess up, use it as a teaching moment instead of a blame - fest.

4. **Be Specific with Feedback.**

Replace vague criticisms like "This isn't good enough" with constructive suggestions like "Here's how we can improve this section." It's not rocket science—it's basic human decency.

5. **Set Boundaries (for Yourself).**

No more emails at midnight. No more weekend texts. Respect your team's time, and they'll respect yours.

6. **Celebrate Wins.**

When your team achieves something, celebrate *them.* Throw a pizza party, write a thank - you note, or just say, "You all did an amazing job." It's not that hard.

7. **Self - Check Regularly.**

Every month, ask yourself: Am I treating my team with respect? Am I giving them the tools they need to succeed? Am I being the kind of boss I'd want to work for? If the answer is no, fix it.

Recovery is a Journey, Not a Destination

Changing your Middle - Finger ways won't happen overnight. You'll slip up. You'll send that unnecessary "just following up" email at 9 p.m. even though you swore you'd stop. You'll micromanage a project without realizing it. Maybe you'll accidentally unleash your inner control freak in a meeting. That's okay. The goal isn't to become a flawless leader—it's to be a *better* one. Progress, not perfection.

And here's the good news: your team isn't secretly plotting your downfall. They don't need you to be a corporate guru or a walking TED Talk. They just want a boss who supports them, trusts them, and doesn't make them want to fake a dentist appointment to avoid coming to work. A little self - awareness goes a long way, and small efforts add up over time.

So, take a deep breath. You've got this. And who knows? Maybe one day, your employees won't instinctively tense up when they see your name in their inbox. Maybe they'll actually laugh at your jokes (instead of out of fear). Maybe—just maybe—they'll stop fantasizing about your sudden career change. Stranger things have happened.

Did This Book Save Your Sanity? Let the World Know!

Well, congratulations - you made it through **Middle-Finger Management** without throwing it across the room in frustration. That's got to count for something. Now, let's talk about something **truly important - your review.**

See that handy QR code over there? **Scan it. Click it. Worship it.** Whatever gets you to Amazon's review page. Why? Because **your feedback helps spread this workplace survival guide to fellow corporate warriors** who are also dodging passive-aggressive emails and surviving pointless meetings.

If this book made you laugh, cry, or rethink your entire career, **give it some stars (preferably five, but hey, no pressure—except there totally is).** Your review **helps expose toxic bosses everywhere—**or at least lets them know we're onto them.

So go ahead, leave a review. **Think of it as your good deed for the day - right up there with pretending to care about the company's latest "team-building" initiative.**

And remember my friends, to keep that attitude of gratitude!

My best,

C.V. Wooster

Amazon Review Link

Visit https://middlefingermanagement.com/

for more information on why your boss stinks.

Now available in an audio version on Audible.com at:

Please check out more books by C. V. Wooster, a man of many talents and a really great boss, we swear!

https://cvwooster.com

And follow the author on all the usual socials . All the links to those, and other C. V. Wooster books are available here at LinkTree.com

More Humor Coming Soon - History: Unattached

What if history's greatest figures had been sent to therapy?

From conquering empires to creating masterpieces, history's most fascinating people weren't just shaped by politics and war—they were also shaped by their relationships, emotional baggage, and, let's be honest, a whole lot of unresolved childhood issues. *History: Unattached* takes a deep (and slightly sarcastic) dive into the attachment styles of legendary figures, exploring how their personal struggles may have influenced the choices that changed the world.

Was Napoleon's thirst for conquest really about proving himself to an indifferent world? Did Joan of Arc's secure attachment help her lead an army? Could Nikola Tesla's anxious-avoidant tendencies explain his self-imposed isolation? And what about those historical enigmas whose attachment styles aren't so easy to pin down?

Through historical analysis, psychological theory, and a touch of humor, *History: Unattached* unpacks the emotional lives of emperors, revolutionaries, artists, and inventors—offering readers a whole new way to look at history. Each chapter explores figures from different walks of life, pairing real biographical details with engaging insights into how attachment theory might help explain their triumphs, mistakes, and relationships.

Think you can diagnose historical figures better than the author? Each chapter ends with a "Your Choice" profile, where readers can put their detective skills to the test. Whether you're a history buff, psychology enthusiast, or just someone who enjoys analyzing people (dead or alive), this book offers a fresh, entertaining way to explore the human side of history.

Get ready to reexamine the past—not through battles and treaties, but through the emotional rollercoaster of some of history's most compelling minds.

https://historyunattached.com